FICTION BY MARGARET J. ANDERSON

Olla-piska: Tales of David Douglas
Children of Summer: Henri Fabre's Insects
The Ghost Inside the Monitor
The Druid's Gift
The Mists of Time
The Brain on Quartz Mountain
Light in the Mountain
The Journey of the Shadow Bairns
In the Circle of Time
Searching for Shona
In the Keep of Time
To Nowhere and Back

Margaret J. Anderson is also the author of 13 nonfiction books for young adults.

FROM A PLACE FAR AWAY
My Scottish Childhood
In World War II

For Yanli —
great to connect with you again!

FROM A PLACE FAR AWAY
My Scottish Childhood In World War II

Margaret J. Anderson

Margaret J. Anderson
December 2017

FROM A PLACE FAR AWAY
My Scottish Childhood
In World War II

Lychgate Press
Copyright © 2017 Margaret J. Anderson
First Edition
All rights reserved

ISBN 13: 978-0-9976116-1-8
ISBN 10: 0-9976116-1-8

Library of Congress Control Number: 2017931704

L Y C H G A T E

editor@lychgatepress.com
www.lychgatepress.com

Front cover: The author with her sister, Ann, and brother, Peter, on the Isle of Skye
Back cover: Head gardener's house, Mertoun Estate

The thistle is the national flower of Scotland.

For my sister Ann

CONTENTS

CHAPTERS

1   In the Beginning... 1
2   The Night the Angel Swore... 7
3   A Tale of Two Thieves... 13
4   Mallaig Mhor... 19
5   More Mallaig Mhor... 25
6   Back to Lockerbie... 33
7   Books and Authors... 39
8   Edinburgh Gran... 45
9   St. Boswells... 53
10   School Days... 61
11   Leading Up to War... 69
12   The Phony War... 77
13   Ann's One... 83
14   The Fever Hospital... 89
15   The House Next Door... 101
16   The War Effort... 109
17   Turning Points... 117
18   Victory... 127
19   A Place Far Away... 135

Acknowledgements

Margaret and John Hall with Peter (age 1), 1929

1

In the Beginning

The year was 1931. Christmas Eve, 1931. The place, Gorebridge, a small coal-mining town a few miles south of Edinburgh. Gorebridge had been hit hard by the Great Depression. Most of the mines were closed and the miners were out of work.

Dr. Edward wearily placed his black bag on the hall table. He'd had a long day without much to show for it. People couldn't afford to pay the grocer, let alone the doctor. He tossed his hat on a shelf, unwound his long woolen scarf, and hung his coat on its peg. He was looking forward to a quiet evening with his wife, eating Christmas cake by the fire and drinking a glass of elderberry wine.

"Is that you, dear?" Bella asked, bustling out of the kitchen to welcome her husband. She'd let the maid go home for Christmas and had made the tea herself. "Mr. Hall, the minister, called," she said. "The baby's on its way."

"How long since he called?" the doctor asked, reaching for his coat.

"Just a few minutes ago. There's time for your tea."

"I could certainly do with a cup."

"Come along then!" As Bella led the way into the dining room, she added, "I'm going to give you your Christmas present a day early. Some people open their presents on Christmas Eve."

"Can't it wait till I'm not so rushed?" Dr. Edward asked.

"No!" Bella said firmly. "I want you to have it before you go over to the Halls."

The doctor drank his tea, ate two scones warm from the griddle, and then began to undo the brightly wrapped package his wife had set by his plate. When he saw what was in it, he stared, first at the present, then at his wife, and then back at the present again, not knowing what to make of it. A miner's lamp. The kind miners wore strapped around their heads to leave their hands free for their coal picks.

"Are you wanting me to change jobs, Bella?" he finally asked.

"Of course not, darling. But you always complain about having to deliver babies in houses where there's nothing brighter than a paraffin lamp. A miner's lamp would shine the light where you needed it and leave your hands free . . ."

"Well . . . yes . . ." Dr. Edward agreed. "It's a really good idea . . . and they don't have electricity at the manse."

So the minister's daughter came into the world on Christmas Eve, dazzled not by the light of a holy star, but by the beam from a miner's lamp. An hour or two earlier, Mrs. Hall had wondered if she was delirious when she heard the midwife saying to a coal miner that he'd taken his time about getting there. "Babies don't wait for people to have their afternoon tea and open their Christmas presents," she said sharply. The coal miner had answered in Dr. Edward's voice, but Mrs. Hall wasn't completely reassured until the baby was finally born. The doctor then unbuckled a bright light from his head and looked like himself again.

"It's a girl! A bonnie wee lass," he told Mr. Hall.

Mr. Hall stood there grinning. He looked too young to be the father of two children, a three-year-old boy, and now a baby girl. There were some in his congregation who thought he looked too young to be a proper minister. They said to one another that young John Hall may have gone to Edinburgh University and studied under the best professors at New College, but with his odd sense of humor and his curly blond hair he didn't act like a minister. Running around the field behind the manse every morning before eating breakfast wasn't how a man of the cloth should start his day. And Mrs. Hall had faddish ideas about programs for the Women's Guild. Besides, she sometimes shopped in Edinburgh instead of spending her money in Gorebridge. How would the Halls feel if people in Gorebridge went off to Edinburgh to go to church?

"I'll wake Peter up to show him his new sister," the excited new father said, still smiling.

Peter was three years old, and had gone to bed thinking about Santa Claus and all the presents he would find in his stocking in the morning. It was very confusing to be wakened in the middle of the night to meet this baby sister. A red-faced, ugly little thing with hardly any hair. And it squeaked even when you didn't squeeze its stomach.

He had asked for a lot of things for Christmas. He was sure a baby sister had not been one of them.

They named the baby Margaret Jean. Peter found she didn't improve much on acquaintance. But his mother seemed to think so. She was forever holding the baby, crooning over her, and calling her funny names. Peter could remember back to the time before this baby was born when his mother called him funny names. Now she mostly called him Peter.

But Peter got even—quite unintentionally. Spring had come, and he and his mother were taking the baby for a walk when they saw two ladies from the church coming towards them.

"Oh, dear! The McDougal sisters," Mrs. Hall said, more to herself than to Peter.

The McDougal sisters never failed to bring up how competent, serious, and Christian the last minister's wife had been. Mrs. Hall glanced down at Margaret Jean lying in her pram, contentedly sucking her thumb, and hoped the baby wouldn't spit up or start to cry.

"So this is the Hall's new little addition," one of the women gushed. Turning to Peter, she asked, "What's your baby sister's name?"

For a three-year-old, Peter had a remarkably clear voice.

"Her name is Margaret Jean," he said. "But Mummy calls her Droonie-Mary-Cookie-Bun."

"Droonie-Mary-Cookie-Bun," the two sisters repeated in horrified unison. "Our last minster and his wife gave their children names that came straight out of the Bible."

Margaret Jean (18 months), 1933

When Peter was five and Margaret Jean was two, the Halls moved to Lockerbie, a small market town in southwest Scotland. The town was a little bigger than Gorebridge, more prosperous, and not so sooty. A year later, Ann was born. It is in Lockerbie that Margaret Jean's story begins. She has no memory of Gorebridge, and no memory of her childhood without Ann at her side.

Margaret Hall with Peter and Margaret Jean in the Manse garden, 1935

2

The Night the Angel Swore

St. Cuthbert's Manse, our new home in Lockerbie, was a big, old house on the edge of town on the road to Dumfries. It had a wonderful garden, hidden behind high hedges and walls. The apple trees, the chestnut tree, and the copper beech were our jungle gym; the shrubbery was marvelous for secret dens and hide-and-seek; and the sloping lawn was where we learned to ride two-wheeler bikes, getting a flying start on the steep grass bank above the lawn.

Before we had bikes, we used to play with an old-fashioned doll's pram we called Jenny. It had belonged to our mother when she was a little girl. She used to take her dolls for sedate walks in Holyrood Park in Edinburgh, but we used Jenny for giving Ann wild rides. Ann was a toddler by this time. We would drag the pram up to the top of the bank, hoist Ann into it, and then give old Jenny a shove. Peter and I would bet on how far the pram would travel before coming to a stop or toppling over. One day, when Peter rode down the hill, poor, tired old Jenny fell to pieces. She'd have been worth something now if we'd taken better care of her!

Peter and Margaret Jean, 1935

Our house had lots of rooms—the study, the sitting room, the playroom, the dining room, the kitchen, the pantry, the scullery, and upstairs bedrooms for everyone, including our maid. High up on one wall in the kitchen was a row of bells that were connected to each room. We children used to amuse ourselves by ringing the bells and racing through the house to see if we could reach the kitchen before the bell stopped clanging.

Although in the early years we always had a live-in maid, it wasn't her job to answer the ringing bells. She was more of a mother's helper and babysitter than a servant. The school leaving age in the 1930s was 14, so girls often got jobs doing housework to put in the years till they were old enough to marry. When Bunty Kilpatrick joined our family, she wasn't much older than Peter. Bunty helped with the housework, the laundry, and kept the fire going in the coal stove, as well as sometimes minding us children. We had no electricity, only coal-gas lights, which had to be lit by long tapers, being careful not to break the fragile mantles. In the evening, my father lit a paraffin lamp on the upstairs landing, and always blew it out before going to bed. After that, the whole house was dark, with no way of getting rid of the darkness because we weren't allowed to have matches.

With so many dark rooms, it was a spooky house. I was glad that Ann and I shared a room. Peter, of course, had a room of his own. One night, thinking it would be fun to scare his little sisters, Peter hid under Ann's bed while we were in the bathroom doing our teeth. After we were snuggled down for the night, he began to wail like a werewolf and shriek like a ghost. We knew it was just Peter and weren't scared at all. But Peter, lying under the bed conjuring up goblins and ghosts, began to think about the long way back to his own room across the empty landing with its creaking boards and flickering shadows. The wailing and screeching wavered to silence.

"Margaret Jean? Ann? Are you awake?" he asked.

"How do you expect us to sleep with you making all that noise?" I asked.

"Will you take me back to my room?"

Ann and I slipped out of our beds. In our long white nightgowns and bare feet, we escorted Peter to his room, one on either side. We even checked under his bed to see that nothing was hiding there.

We all had blond hair like our father. Usually, before going to bed at night, Mother brushed Ann's and my hair and braided it into tight pigtails. One evening, she told Ann and me that we'd have to brush our own hair. The church elders and their wives were coming to dinner.

"Can we stay up and see the people?" I asked.

"Not this time. Off you go to bed, and I don't want to hear a peep out of any of you till morning."

We usually had dinner in the middle of the day—soup, meat, potatoes, and vegetables, followed by pudding. Late in the afternoon, we had tea—sandwiches and cakes and biscuits and milk. After the children were in bed, our parents ate supper by themselves. Quite often, enticed by the smell of frying bacon or warm gingerbread, we'd creep downstairs and beg "just one bite."

That evening, with all those important guests coming, the cooking smells were extra inviting. I couldn't fall asleep. I heard the doorknocker several times, followed by the rumble of the men's voices and the lighter, laughing voices of the women.

Silence followed, and then the sound of voices again as the visitors crossed the hall on their way to the dining room to feast on all that good-smelling food.

I slipped out of bed and ran down to the turn in the stairs that overlooked the front hall. The visitors looked up and saw me. I stood there in my white nightgown, with my long, fair hair loose around my shoulders.

"What a little angel!" one of the ladies breathed. "Isn't she precious?"

I smiled shyly. It was working! In a minute, they'd invite me to come down and they'd give me a piece of cake.

But my mother shattered the dream.

"Margaret Jean Hall! You get back to bed this instant!"

I was furious. All these people down there making so much noise I couldn't sleep, and eating our good food and not letting me have any. Quite suddenly, a word that Peter had used just the day before popped into my head. I knew from the way he looked when he said it that it was a satisfying thing to call someone. I leaned over the bannister and said in a ringing voice, "You're all a lot of buggers."

The church ladies and gentlemen looked horrified, but my father burst out laughing. Pretty soon everyone else joined in, perhaps a little uncertainly. I turned and ran back up to bed and buried my head under the pillow. Being laughed at was just about as bad a punishment as I could imagine.

And the laughter went on for years. The night of the supper party became one of my father's favorite stories. The night the angel swore.

Margaret Jean and Ann, 1937

3

A Tale of Two Thieves

Old Miss Hadley was blind and didn't get out much, so she always looked forward to my father's pastoral visits. She loved to hear about what his children were up to.

"Bring them over to see me," she begged. "I miss having bairns around."

So the next time my father went to see the old lady he took Ann and me along. I sat on a chair, swinging my feet, and answered Miss Hadley's questions about school. Ann, who was around four, was too young to go to school and too shy to say anything. She poked around the room, looking at the ornaments. On a low shelf, she spotted a little white china rabbit with pink ears, one pointing up, the other flopping over. Ann fell in love with that rabbit.

When it was finally time to leave, we said our goodbyes to Miss Hadley and followed Father down the garden path. As he closed the gate, he reached for Ann's hand, and was met by a tightly closed fist.

"What have you got there?" he asked.

Ann opened her hand and showed him the little white rabbit.

"Did you take that from Miss Hadley's house?" he asked sternly.

Ann nodded. Then she smiled happily and said, "It's all right, Daddy. She's blind. She didn't see me."

Some time later, Ann redeemed herself, at least in my eyes. Mrs. Moffat, one of my father's parishioners had invited us all for tea. She proudly served each of us a small helping of raspberries fresh from her garden. When Ann finished popping the raspberries into her mouth one by one, she noticed a tiny green caterpillar walking around the rim of her plate. She figured Mrs. Moffat would be mortified when she cleared away the dishes and realized she'd served her guests a caterpillar along with the raspberries, so Ann valiantly scooped up the little green worm and swallowed it.

When my own children were young, and were picky about their food, I used to tell them how Ann cleaned her plate down to the last caterpillar. They were not impressed.

When Ann stole the rabbit, I'm sure our father made her return it. But when I lapsed into thievery, nobody made me give anything back, because nobody knew. Except Ann—and maybe, God.

On Sunday mornings, my father always shut himself up in his study. If you listened at the door, you could hear him mumbling away, delivering his sermon to an empty room. He didn't need to remind us to be quiet. The entire house had that Sunday feel. If we forgot that it was the Sabbath and clattered down the stairs or scuffled in the hall, he would bang his fist on the study door and we immediately fell silent. All week he was approachable and friendly, pliable as clay, but on Sundays, he was granite. He wore a black suit and a black top hat, and he wore a flowing black robe in the pulpit.

St. Cuthbert's Church, Lockerbie

Our family had a pew near the front of the church that ran sideways to the rest of the seats. If we children fidgeted or giggled, everyone in the congregation could see us. For some reason that made Ann and me want to giggle all the more, especially if anything out of line happened like Peter sneezing or Ann dropping her hymnbook. It was always a relief when the morning service was safely over.

We attended church again in the evening, but that service was somehow different from the morning one. The church was dimly lit—quiet and holy—and warm, because the furnace had been on all day. Most of the pews were empty, and the slow notes of the organ drowned out our voices as we sang the hymns.

The day Thou gavest, Lord, has ended
The darkness falls at Thy behest.
To Thee our morning hymns ascended.
Thy peace shall sanctify our rest.

After church we all walked home together and ate supper in the kitchen by the fire, listening to a serial on the wireless. Books by Sir Walter Scott and Charles Dickens. Books that sang like the words in the Bible.

Separating the morning and evening services was the long afternoon when the quietness rule still held. Part of the afternoon was spent in Sunday school. To get to St. Cuthbert's Church from our house you had to go up the hill to the town, past the shops, the town hall, the picture house, and then over the railway bridge. By the time Ann started Sunday school, I was considered old enough and reliable enough to take her.

The best thing about Sunday school was learning Bible verses. They were printed on small cards with pictures of birds or flowers, and if you could say the verse by heart, you were rewarded with a new verse to learn. The other big moment was taking the collection. One child was chosen to stand at the end of the hall holding a velvet bag with wooden handles, while the rest of us marched around the room, singing:

> *Hear the pennies dropping,*
> *listen while they fall.*
> *Every one for Jesus, he shall have them all.*
> *Dropping, dropping, dropping, dropping,*
> *Hear the pennies fall.*
> *Every one for Jesus, he shall have them all.*

It was like the musical games we played at birthday parties.

Although I went to church twice on Sundays, and to Sunday school in the afternoon, I didn't spend a lot of time thinking about God, but when I did, I found it rather worrying. God being everywhere and knowing everything wasn't comforting. And didn't seem possible. I didn't see how He could know what we were up to all the time. Parents were quicker to set you right than God was. I decided to put the matter to the test. If God knew you'd been naughty, what would He do about it?

"I'm not going to put any money in the collection bag today," I whispered to Ann, as we approached the church hall. A penny was flat on my palm inside my glove.

"Are you just going to keep the penny?" Ann asked.

"I'm going to spend it on sweeties!"

"It's Jesus' money," Ann reminded me primly.

"How's he going to know?" I answered. "It'll be easy. I'll just walk past the collection bag as if I'd forgotten to bring any money."

It wasn't easy.

Wee Jimmy Johnson had been chosen to hold the collection bag, but the Sunday school superintendent was standing right next to him. The superintendent was a tall, thin man with bushy eyebrows and piercing, black eyes that could see everything. I clenched my fist around the penny inside my glove and marched right past the collection bag.

After Sunday school, Ann and I ran all the way to the stationer's shop.

"A penny worth o' toffees," I said, handing over the coin in my glove.

Once we were outside, I shared them with Ann.

"Are you going to buy sweeties next Sunday, too?" Ann asked hopefully.

I shook my head. They didn't taste all that good. And now when I thought about God, He had bushy eyebrows and piercing black eyes.

4

Mallaig Mhor

Scotland is divided into three parts—the Highlands, the Midlands, and the Lowlands. The Highlanders live in fishing villages or lonely little farms called crofts, which nestle between high mountains, close to roaring rivers, or near beaches of silver sand. The Midlanders live in towns and cities, amidst shops and factories and parks and coal mines. The Lowlands consist of farm country and small towns. We were Lowlanders for eleven months of the year, but in the other month, August, our family went to Mallaig Mhor and became Highlanders. From the ring of the name, you can tell that being a Highlander is best. There is a wildness and strangeness about the Highlands that gave the month of August "another time, another place" sort of feel.

Mallaig Mhor is a croft in a bay on Loch Nevis, a narrow inlet of the sea, north of the fishing town of Mallaig. The croft lies beyond the last station on the railway line and beyond the end of the road. The only way to get there is by boat, or by hiking through the heather over a mountain.

The first time we went there, Ann was still a baby. We arrived at Mallaig Station, with piles of luggage—enough to see us through the month. Donald MacDonald from Mallaig Mhor was waiting on the platform to meet us, dressed in a raincoat and sou'wester. We didn't know it then, but only in the wildest weather did Donald bother with a raincoat. The rest of the time, he wore a dark blue jersey and a flat gray cap.

"I have the boat waiting," he said politely. "We'd better hurry because there's weather on the way."

We should have been warned as to what lay ahead when we heard Donald urging us to hurry. Highlanders live by the pace of the tide and milking time, and seldom see any need to hurry. And there was that word, "weather." In the Lowlands, there was weather every day—good, bad, or indifferent. In the Highlands, "weather" had only one meaning.

Heads down and shoulders hunched against the driving rain, we left the shelter of the station and made our way to the pier. A rowboat, with an oily outboard motor dangling over the stern, was fighting at its mooring at the bottom of a flight of stone steps, slick with spray and seaweed. Willing hands helped with our luggage. By the time everything and everyone had been stowed on board, the boat settled low in the water.

"She rides better with a good load," Donald said softly, pulling on the cord to start the outboard motor.

A number of old fishermen watched from the pier, sucking on unlit pipes and balefully shaking their heads. My parents were beginning to think it might have been wiser to spend the night at the Station Hotel, but just then the engine sparked to life. They watched nervously as the ribbon of black water widened between the boat and the pier.

At first, the boat moved along sturdily, sliding over the swell, but as soon as we were beyond the shelter of the harbor, she went wild, bucking every wave. I sat in the prow, hanging onto the sides, licking salt spray from my cheeks. I counted the waves. Every seventh wave was supposed to be bigger than the rest, but it was hard to tell when to start counting with the waves falling on us like collapsing mountains. No one thought of life jackets for children or for grownups back then.

Ann, who tended to get car sick, turned green. My mother's face was white. But I found it rather exhilarating, though I did panic a bit when the others in the boat began to shift places and the boat rocked sideways as well as up and down. The waves were pushing us horribly close to a jagged headland, where the sea was smashing against the rocks, sending white plumes of spray up into the clouds to join the driving rain. Donald and my father grabbed a set of oars and fitted them into the rowlocks. It was then that I realized the outboard motor had died. With the noise of the wind and the waves, I hadn't noticed that the chugging engine had stopped.

We finally inched our way past the rocks. Beyond the next headland, the waves were no longer quite so wild. Donald turned the boat toward the shore, and there was Mallaig Mhor, like a painting in a book. A little white house, sitting squarely in the middle of closely cropped green turf. A short distance up the hillside on our left was a low stone building with a roof of corrugated tin—a two room house known as a but-an'-ben—that shared a wall with the byre.

The house had been the MacDonald's home until the early 1930s when the government stepped in and built modern homes for crofters in hopes of stopping the flow of people from the Highlands to the cities. Now, some crofters, including the MacDonald's, made a little extra money in the summer months by moving back to their old, dilapidated houses and renting the new homes to holidaymakers from the south. So, while we occupied the white cottage with its Aga cooker and indoor plumbing, the MacDonalds spent the summer in the two-roomed but-an'-ben. Their family consisted of the old mother and her three grown children—Duncan, Donald and Morag. I don't remember a father.

When the rowboat crunched to a stop in the sand, my father grabbed me before I shot over the prow. Waves swished around us, and the boat rocked wildly when Donald jumped into the shallow water. We all had to wade to get to dry land, but it didn't matter because we were already soaking wet.

Mallaig Mhor, photo by Alan Reid

"Morag will have the fire going and a cup of tea waiting," Donald told my mother, as she splashed ashore clutching Ann tightly in her arms. "Go on up to the house now. I'll have my brother help me with the luggage."

Morag ushered us in, smiling shyly. The house smelled of varnish and seashells. I was soon seated on a stool next to the kitchen table, which was covered with green and white oilcloth, cautiously sipping a cup of strong, sweet tea. I never got to have tea at home.

"It's hot," I said.

"Pour it into your saucer to let it cool a wee bit," Morag told me, as if drinking tea from a saucer was the most usual thing in the world.

The next morning, the sun was shining and the beach was littered with debris from the storm. While we were beachcombing, a boat from Mallaig came into the bay.

"It'll be bringing our coal," my father told us.

The boat anchored some distance from the shore. "They're dumping our coal in the sea," Peter shouted. "Look at that! They're dumping it in the sea!"

"That's how they deliver it here," my father said calmly. "There's no dock, so they can't bring the boat in any closer. When the tide goes out, we'll fetch the coal up to the house."

The Highlands was indeed a strange, Alice-in-Wonderland sort of place.

Peter, Margaret Jean, and Ann, 1938

5

More Mallaig Mhor

Back in Lockerbie, the milk was delivered to our front door in glass bottles, but at Mallaig Mhor Peter and I had to fetch the milk each morning at milking time from the MacDonald's byre. It was delivered into our white jug, warm and frothy, straight from the cow. If Donald happened to be doing the milking, he'd squirt milk right into our open mouths. I didn't really care for the warm milk, but I was too polite to say so.

Sometimes we visited old Mrs. MacDonald in her dark little house right next the byre. Through the wall, you could hear the cows gently moving in their stalls at milking time. You could smell them, too. I loved the old house. It was like being inside the pages of a fairly tale. Even on the warmest day, old Mrs. MacDonald sat in a rocking chair near the peat fire, bundled up in woolen cardigans and shawls. She only spoke Gaelic, so Peter and I didn't understand a word she said, but her voice was like music and the words a magic spell. Sometimes she and Morag would talk together. Morag would then ask us a question and, turning back to the old woman, she'd speak Gaelic again. Mrs. MacDonald would nod and laugh, her single tooth gleaming in the firelight. She was a witch, but a kindly witch. She sometimes gave us toffees that were soft and gooey and stuck to the paper wrappers.

Another part of the magic of Mallaig Mhor was the old record player in the front room. A wind-up gramophone with a pile of Harry Lauder records. By the end of the holidays we knew all the words to *Just a wee Deoch an' Doris* and *Roamin' in the Gloamin'*. But our mother didn't like us hugger-muggering by the fire with old Mrs. MacDonald or playing records in the front room when we could be outside getting fresh air. My mother was big on fresh air. If she were alive today, she wouldn't approve of her great grandchildren hugger-muggering indoors with their iPads and smart phones.

So most of our time was spent outdoors, climbing the heather-clad hills, or playing on the beach, poking about in rock pools, and splashing in the waves. Close to the shore, baby flounders wriggled under our bare feet. Mallaig is a long way north, but the temperature of the water is modified by the Gulf Stream and we never seemed to feel cold.

One afternoon, when the sea was calm, we borrowed spears from the MacDonalds and went out after flounders in the shallow water of the bay at low tide. I don't remember ever catching any. The spear seemed to change directions when it went into the water, and the flounders were hard to see because they blended with the speckled sand. I didn't want to spear one anyway. It seemed more cruel than snagging spotted mackerel on a fishing line behind the boat.

Another afternoon, we rowed across Loch Nevis to Knoydart and spent the afternoon looking for tiny cowrie shells on a white sandy beach. On the way back, a group of curious seals surrounded the boat, coming so close that we could look into their round brown eyes and count their whiskers.

"They're bumping against the boat," I said, clutching Ann. "They're going to knock it over."

"They're only curious," Mother said. "Here in the Highlands they call them 'the selkie folk.' They've been known to save drowning sailors. And if you ever come across a sealskin on the beach, you must leave it there, because it belongs to a seal who has become human for a while and he'll die if he can't find his skin when he wants to return to the sea."

Looking over the side of the boat at their gentle, comical faces, I was reassured.

Farther up Loch Nevis, a small island nestled against the shore. It looked so much like part of the mainland that you could row right past it, not knowing that it was an island. Father told us that after the Jacobite Rebellion in 1745, Bonnie Prince Charlie escaped from the English soldiers by rowing behind the island up the narrow channel. The soldiers who were pursuing him kept on up Loch Nevis, while Prince Charlie doubled back and escaped over the sea to Skye.

Peter and Margaret Jean with their parents on holiday at Mallaig Mhor, 1935

Peter, Ann, and I spent many happy hours playing at being Bonnie Prince Charlie hiding from the English on the heather-clad hill behind the house. When we accompanied our father on the long hike over the hills into Mallaig to buy groceries, it helped to pretend we were Jacobites dodging enemy soldiers. But we morphed back into tourists when we reached Mallaig and sat on the harbor wall licking ice cream cones.

For Mother and us children Sundays were like any other day, but Father usually attended the little white church in Mallaig. One Sunday, he set off over the hill, compass in hand, planning to go to a church in a village several miles down the coast. It was a warm day and he wore hiking boots and shorts. When he finally reached the church, the sound of the organ told him that the service had already started. He felt a little awkward about walking in late since he was so casually dressed. In those days men wore dark suits to church, especially in the Highlands, and the women and girls all wore dresses and hats.

When he spied a narrow door at the rear of the building, he thought he would be able to slip in unnoticed. The door opened into a passage with a short flight of steps at the end, leading to another door. Quietly opening the second door, my father stepped inside—and found himself standing in the pulpit next to the minister!

Being a minister himself, he was used to seeing the congregation from up above, but never before had he looked down on so many astonished faces. When he came home, he turned his misadventure into a funny story, but I knew he must have felt terrible, standing there in his open-necked shirt and hiking boots and shorts.

It made me think of a dream I sometimes had. I'd be in school, and I'd look down and find I was still wearing my pajamas. All the children would point at me and laugh. The people probably didn't laugh in church, but I bet they couldn't stop laughing when they told everyone later about the hiker who nearly knocked the minister out of his pulpit.

Ann, Margaret Jean, and Peter, 1937

6

Back to Lockerbie

When we returned to Lockerbie our parents became submerged in their own busy worlds. Father had his parishioners to worry about and his sermons to write. Mother, with the help of the maid, coped with the endless chores of running the household. Doing the laundry without a washing machine. Pinning clothes on the wash line in good weather, and hanging them on the pulleys in the kitchen when it rained. Heating flat irons by the fire and cooking on the coal-fired kitchen stove. Walking up the hill to the town to do the shopping every day. We called it "going the messages." We didn't have a car.

This gave Ann and me a lot of freedom to explore the nearby fields and woods. We became adept at scrambling up onto our back wall and jumping down into what we called the back field. That was where we used to roll our hard-boiled eggs down the grassy hillside on Easter Monday. We colored the eggs with onion skins or gorse blossoms. When we were rolling them, if they hit a stone and cracked, we peeled the marbled shell and ate the eggs. Rolling the eggs symbolized rolling the stone away from Jesus' tomb. I tried to introduce the tradition to my grandchildren, but it didn't catch on! They would sooner hunt for chocolate eggs.

To the west of the back field was a magical no-man's land we called the Boggy Bit. At some point a farmer had tried to drain the Boggy Bit, so it was crossed by rows of parallel ditches that drained into a marshy area, where we once found the decaying body of a sheep. The next time we went to look for it, it was gone. We assumed it had been sucked down into the mud, so after that we steered clear of the marsh. It might suck us in, too.

Sometimes there were cows in the back field. This gave an element of overcoming danger to claim our enchanted land. The cows would follow us, thinking we'd come to feed them. Or maybe they were just curious. But when we arrived at the twisted hedge that separated the Boggy Bit from the field, braving the cows was always worth it. Some of the old trees had bent trunks so you could ride them like a pony, and in the spring, the Boggy Bit was ablaze with color—daisies and buttercups, pink ragged robin, and golden marsh marigolds. The ditches were filled with little critters we could collect in jam jars. Some of the ditches had plank bridges, where we would lie on our stomachs dabbling our hands in the muddy water. We jumped across the narrower ditches, sometimes misjudging and ending up with wet feet.

The Boggy Bit was a source of material for our museum. We'd set up the museum in an old washhouse that stood in the corner of our garden. Before our time, it was where the maid did the weekly washing, boiling clothes in a huge metal tub over a coal fire. There were two deep, rusty sinks, where we raised tadpoles from spawn we brought home from the ditches. We loved watching the tadpoles grow legs and transform into miniature frogs. We pressed flowers between sheets of blotting paper, and had a collection of stones and bones. On at least one occasion the museum became home to an injured hedgehog that we found at the edge of the road. I seem to remember that our humanitarian venture ended with a hedgehog funeral.

Ann and I were fond of earwigs. Near the front door was a flowerbed where Mother had planted poppies. When they finished blooming, the seed heads turned out to be a hiding place for earwigs. We broke off the heads and carefully carried them over to the front door step. The step was formed from two slabs of sandstone with a fairly wide crack between them. We tapped the seed heads on the step chasing out the earwigs and then herded them to the crack, where they plunged down into the darkness. We imagined them all living together in a happy earwig city under our front step.

One morning we wandered farther than usual from home down Dumfries Road and found ourselves following a wide path cut through the Cemetery Woods—probably a fire break. The plantation of conifer trees rose tall on either side, cutting out the light. We wondered where the path would take us.

"What's that noise?' Ann asked, looking anxious.

We stopped and listened. There was no mistaking the sound—the distant baying of hounds. I grabbed Ann's hand and we began to run back towards the road. On occasion we'd watched the hunt gather in the town square, and had loved seeing all those men and women sitting astride their tall horses in their smart red coats with restless dogs weaving between the horses' hooves. But it would be a lot different seeing them at full gallop in the woods. And the dogs might forget that they were following the scent of a fox. If they caught up with us, they'd surely tear us to pieces. The red-coated men and women might not see us in time to call off the hounds. When Ann stumbled, I yanked her to her feet, urging her to run faster. I had a stitch in my side, but we daren't slow down.

We reached the safely of the road before the hounds caught us. In fact, walking up the road, away from the confines of the wood, we could scarcely hear them. The fox must have led them off in another direction. But for a long time I could hear those hounds baying in my dreams. I never again went to see the hunt assemble in the town square, but that may have been because the war put an end to fox hunting.

Our adventure with the hounds gave me some empathy for foxes that I hadn't felt until then, perhaps because, when I was around the age of five, I had a bad experience with a fox. It happened within the covers of a book. To celebrate the fact that I had mastered reading, my grandmother sent me a little book featuring Danny Duck. The book started out quite innocently with Danny Duck saying goodbye to his mother duck and setting off for school. He had his schoolbag slung over one wing and a jaunty little blue school cap on his head. On page four you could see happy little Danny waddling along. On the opposite page, half hidden by a tree, was a leering fox. I didn't need to turn the page to know what the next picture would show.

A lot of blood and feathers and no more Danny Duck!

I tried several times to read that book, but I never had the courage to go beyond page five. So one day, with Ann's help, I ripped the book apart. Ann was two years old—a good age for ripping the pages to pieces. When we'd finished, we flushed that leering fox and poor Danny Duck down the toilet. Our toilet had a cistern up near the ceiling and you pulled a chain to release a flood of water into the toilet bowl. It was very satisfying to watch the ripped-up pages swirl around and then finally gurgle off to we knew not where.

When we'd finished, we realized we had a problem. What to do with the cover? It was too sturdy to tear apart and flush down the toilet. In the end I just put it back in the bookcase in our bedroom. The wicked fox no longer lurked in its pages.

Several nights later, Mother came upstairs to read us our bedtime story. She was in a hurry that evening, so she chose the thinnest book in the bookcase. She was surprised—and then upset—when she found it had no pages.

Books were right up there with fresh air in my mother's mind.

Destroying a book—any book—was a sin. And getting Ann to help me tear up books was an added sin. I tried to explain about the blood and feathers, but my mother was in no mood to listen. What would Gran say when she heard what I'd done to the lovely book she'd sent me? What was I thinking about, teaching Ann to rip out all the pages? My mother's angry words swirled around my head like the scraps of paper in the toilet bowl. It was, however, comforting to picture Danny Duck with his jaunty school cap bobbing about on some distant river after a rough ride down the toilet, while that mean old fox drowned.

7

Books and Authors

Several of the books on the shelves in our bedroom dated back to my mother's childhood. They tended to be rather moral, and often sad. I remember sobbing over young Ada's death in *Ada and Gertie*. My mother had wept for Ada a generation earlier. Elnora Comstock's mother was mean beyond belief in *A Girl of the Limberlost*. Poor Judy Abbott, who wrote an entire book of letters to Daddy Long Legs, spent her childhood in the dreary John Grier Orphanage. In *What Katy Did*, after being warned not to play on the swing in the woodshed, Katy Carr fell and injured her spine, leaving her bedridden for the next 60 pages.

These last three books were all by American authors, but I don't think their American setting broadened my horizons, because I imagined all the action happening in our back yard. Ann and I spent hours acting out the stories, pretending to be the different characters. We especially loved the Carr family in the Katy books. Being the oldest, I always got to be tomboy Katy and Ann had to settle on being gentle Clover or whiny Elsie. We had our own version of the Carr children's "Paradise" under the rhododendron bushes at the bottom of the garden, where we ate secret feasts. The Boggy Bit was our Limberlost, though we never found a Luna moth or a Yellow Empress.

For years our favorite books were Rupert Bear books by Mary Tourtel—little yellow hardbacks with black and white drawings. Rupert lived in Nutwood, an idyllic English village, where he went on adventures with his many friends, including Bill Badger and Edward Trunk, an elephant. The stories were told in rhyming couplets. There were 46 books in the series, and by the time Ann and I had outgrown the stories, we owned most of them, thanks to the generosity of Edinburgh Gran.

Rupert is coming up on his hundredth birthday. He started out as a comic strip in the

Daily Express in 1920 and it's still running. A color version, the Rupert Bear Annual, has been published every year since 1936, even during the war years, when paper was scarce. Rupert was credited with boosting the British morale. More recently he has continued his adventures in videos and computer games. But for me Rupert belongs inside the covers of those magical little yellow books.

Two other books provided us with a lot of fun. One was *Gone is Gone* by Wanda Gág. The other was a book of children's sermons. It wasn't the content of those books that we loved. It was the names of the authors. Just saying "Wanda Gág" made us collapse on the bed in a fit of the giggles. The book of sermons was given to us by a minister friend of my father's. He had the unfortunate name of Edgar Primrose Dickie. Edgar Dickie would have been bad enough. How had Edgar *Primrose* Dickie survived his schooldays and lived long enough to write a book?

Annie S. Swan is another author whose name has stayed with me all these years although I never read any of her books. Probably because she wrote romantic novels with a Christian leaning—around 150 of them—and I was in my Rupert Bear phase when I met her. She was an early suffragist and ran for Parliament in the General Election in 1922. In 1930, she was awarded the Commander of the British Empire for her literary achievements. I have no idea how this Famous

Author came to be opening a garden fête in our manse garden in 1935, but I do remember bumping heads with her.

St. Cuthbert's Manse

Each summer, the church held a fête in the manse garden to raise money to help pay the minister's salary. It was a long-standing tradition. There were pony rides on the wash green and various stalls set up on the front lawn. My favorites were the beanbag toss, the bottle stall, and the bake sale. Afternoon tea was served on wobbly card tables under the apple trees. As the great day approached, my rising excitement must have been matched by my parents' rising anxiety! The bushes had to be trimmed, the lawn mowed, and the paths weeded. How many people would show up? Had they made enough pots of tea and ordered enough lemonade? And would the sun shine? Planning an outdoor event in Scotland is a chancy business. The saying goes that if you can't see the hills it's raining, and if you can see the hills, then it's going to rain. The anxiety level that year must have been exceptionally high with the Famous Author coming.

When the great day finally arrived the sun shone. Crowds of people came. Annie S. Swan got there on time. She was a very old lady, but that's what you'd expect after writing over 150 books. While she made her opening remarks, I stood quietly next to my mother, who was holding a huge bouquet. On my other side was one of the church ladies. My hair was well brushed and I was wearing a pretty new dress with a full skirt made from a light, flowery material. Gran had sent it from Edinburgh because I had an important role to play that afternoon. I was to say thank you to the Famous Author at the end of her talk and present her with the bunch of flowers.

The talk was winding down when the church lady whispered to me that she liked my dress. Eager to respond to the compliment, I lifted the skirt up over my face and told her, "Aye, and it's got knickers tae match!"

At that moment, Annie S. Swan said, "I declare this Fête open!" which was my cue to walk forward with the flowers. All eyes turned in my direction as my mother quickly flipped my skirt back down, handed me the bouquet and pushed me forward.

When I reached the old lady I whispered, "Thank you!" and I handed her the flowers. Feeling I needed to do something more, I spread my skirt and did a deep curtsey. Annie S. Swan must also have felt the occasion called for something more. Just as I bobbed up from my curtsey, she leaned forward to give me a kiss, and that's how I bumped heads with a Famous Author.

8

Edinburgh Gran

Our grandmother on my mother's side lived in Edinburgh. We called her Edinburgh Gran to distinguish her from my father's mother, St. Boswells Gran. As you might guess, she lived in St. Boswells, a small border town on the River Tweed.

Although Lockerbie is closer to St. Boswells than to Edinburgh, Edinburgh was easier to reach by train. So that Gran played a bigger role in our lives. On several occasions, I got to stay with Edinburgh Gran on my own.

Visiting Edinburgh, with its castle, museums, tea shops, tramcars, and zoo was like visiting a city on another planet. I especially remember going to the zoo, where I had to see everything. And it had to be timed so that we were there when the penguins were taken out of their cage for their daily walk, and when the lions were fed, and when the chimpanzees sat around a little table enjoying a rambunctious tea party.

By then, Gran's feet were hurting, so she bought me a ticket for an elephant ride and sank down into a lawn chair. Then she paid for another ride, and another . . . I got to ride that elephant seven times, perched on the wooden saddle, sitting sideways, surrounded by squirming children. By the seventh ride, I was growing a bit bored. I stared at the elephant's gray wrinkled skin. Leaning forward, I yanked on one of its sparse hairs. The elephant responded by raising its trunk and trumpeting. The sound was extraordinary—louder than the castle gun that was fired each day at one o'clock. I'm sure it echoed all over Edinburgh and out across the Firth of Forth till it reached the distant ships at sea. The children near me began to whimper. When the elephant paused at the unloading platform I was the first to scramble down. I raced over to Gran, praying that the angry beast wouldn't come stampeding after me.

Gran suggested it was time to go home, and I grabbed her hand and dragged her toward the tram stop. Usually, I insisted on going upstairs, hoping to get a front seat so that I could pretend to be driving the tram along the tracks, but today all I wanted was to be invisible. When the tram came, I slunk into a seat downstairs.

Gran must have noticed I was upset, because she tried to cheer me up by telling about a funny incident that had happened long ago when my mother was a little girl. I'd heard it many times before because it was one of my mother's favorite stories, but it still made me laugh when Gran told it. One morning, she and my mother climbed aboard the tram and took their seats. Opposite them sat a woman and a young boy, both staring straight ahead. The odd thing was that the lad had a chamber pot stuck on his head. He was dressed in his school uniform. And perched on top of the pot was the boy's school cap! Still staring straight ahead, they got off the tram at the Royal Infirmary. My mother always finished her version of the story by saying, "Somewhere, at this very moment, there's a boy of about your age saying to his father, 'Daddy, Daddy, tell me the story about when you were a wee laddie and had to go to the Infirmary to get the doctor to pry the pottie off your head'." Then my brother Peter would add, "I hope the pottie was empty when the boy stuck his head in it!"

By the time we got back to Gran's house on Willowbrae Avenue, I had recovered from being afraid of the elephant. But there was one animal that I never did get over being scared of—the tiger that lived in Gran's front parlor. The parlor was upstairs with its windows looking out on the street. Across the hall was my bedroom, a small room facing the walled back garden, which was just a patch of overgrown grass and was nothing like our garden back home. When it was time for bed, I always made sure the door to the parlor was tightly shut, because I didn't want the tiger creeping across the hall and invading my dreams.

During the day, especially when Ann was staying at Gran's house too, we'd open the parlor door and peak in at the tiger. Its beady, unblinking glass eyes stared back at us. Its mouth was wide open, showing

The Edinburgh grandparents, William and Margaret Reid, with Peter, Ann, and Margaret on the Isle of Skye, 1939

all its fierce teeth. Its gleaming skin stretched over the back of the sofa, as if ready to pounce. When we asked Gran why she had a tiger in the front room, she told us it was a present from Uncle Alex. Alex was my mother's younger brother, who lived in India. I hoped he'd never decide to bring a tiger back to his sister.

Our grandfather, William Reid, was a rather shadowy figure. He was the Sports Editor for the Edinburgh Evening News and wrote under the name of Diogenes. He wasn't around much, but on Saturday mornings he would say in his gruff voice, "This is the day the ghost walks!" and hand each of us a penny. He also ate prunes along with his porridge at breakfast time, which struck me as so weird that I can still see him slurping up his prunes after all these years.

My grandmother was a McLean. Her family moved from the Highlands to the city when she was a baby. As a child, she lived in the Cannongate at the bottom of the Royal Mile, in what we would call low-cost housing, but then it was a slum. The house is no longer there. Ironically, that historic district is now expensive real estate. Gran was so ashamed of her background that when my mother was little, she was never taken to visit her grandmother in the ramshackle house on the High Street.

When Gran finished school, she got a job as a reader for Nelson, the publisher. Then she met the young newspaper reporter, William Reid. She was so committed to her children rising up the social ladder that my mother was given elocution lessons for years as a child and then attended Edinburgh Ladies' College, a private school. She went on to Edinburgh University where she met and married young John Hall. I think Gran would have liked her daughter to marry someone with better economic prospects—ministers were not well paid—but my parents were at least assured of a roof over their heads in the post-depression years.

My mother passed the fruits of her elocution lessons on to the next generation. We all learned to recite, with great sensitivity, Hillaire Belloc's poem about poor Jim who ran away from his nurse at the zoo and was eaten by a lion. This may have accounted for my fear of the tiger.

> *There was a Boy whose name was Jim;*
> *His friends were very good to him,*
> *They gave him Tea, and Cakes, and Jam,*
> *And slices of delicious Ham,*
> *And Chocolate with pink inside*
> *And little Tricycles to ride,*
> *And read him stories through and through,*
> *And even took him to the Zoo—*

It was there that Jim slipped away from his nurse and the unfortunate boy was eaten by a lion which . . .

> *. . . hungrily began to eat*
> *the Boy: beginning at his feet.*
> *Now just imagine how it feels*
> *When first your toes and then your heels,*
> *And then by gradual degrees,*
> *Your shins and ankles, calves and knees,*
> *Are slowly eaten bit by bit.*
> *No wonder Jim detested it!*

My mother insisted that we children speak the King's English. Which we mostly did. We became sort of bilingual, speaking "properly" at home and lapsing into the border dialect with the children at school. It was important to blend in when you were playing peavery beds (hopscotch) in the school playground. At home you *didn't know*, but at school you *didna' ken;* at home you *didn't worry,* but at school you *didna fash yersel';* at home you said *thanks* and at school you said *Ta!* But at both home and school, when you waved goodbye, you always said, "*Ta-ta!*" That sounds strange to my ears now.

9

St. Boswells

Although St. Boswells had no zoo with elephant rides nor a tiger in the parlor, it had its own attractions. My St. Boswells grandparents owned a sweetie shop. It was actually the village Tobacco and News paper Shop, but we weren't interested in cigarettes and newspapers. What did interest us were the sparkling glass jars of barley sugar and humbugs and liquorice allsorts. My grandfather was a tall, lean man, but I have no clear memory of my grandmother. Maybe she spent all her time in the kitchen preparing meals for us while we explored the surrounding countryside and played with our cousins, George and Ian, who lived a few doors away.

    A big attraction was the St. Boswells Fair, which takes place on the village green each year on July 18th. The Fair dates back to the 17th century. In bygone days it was a gathering place for gypsies from all over the south of Scotland, who traded horses and told fortunes. St. Boswells had its own resident gypsy, a rather scary old woman who went from door to door selling brushes, earning her the name Scrubber Liz.

By the time we attended the Fair, it was a scaled down version of what it had once been, with fewer gypsies and horses and more rides for children. But there were enough gambling stalls to teach me a life lesson. Our grandfather had given each of us a shilling to spend at the Fair. That was a generous amount of money back then, enough to keep us busy for most of the day. Soon after we arrived at the village green, I got separated from Ann and the cousins. I assumed they had headed for the rides, but I didn't go looking for them. Wide-eyed, I wandered among the booths. All those prizes to win and so many ways to double your money. I pictured myself joining the others with my arms full of stuffed animals, staggering under the weight of the pennies in my pockets.

Of course, it didn't work out that way. My aim was off when I threw balls at skittles and I wasn't close to the bull's eye when I shot at a target. It looked so easy to double your money on the bagatelle board, but the ball just wobbled into the gutter. In my panic to win back some money I tried again . . . and again. I couldn't believe it when I reached into my pocket for another penny and found that my money was gone. I went off in search of Ann and Ian. When I found them, I told them I'd lost my money. They offered to help me look for it, but I just shrugged. I couldn't bring myself to explain how I'd lost it. Ann offered to pay for a ride on the merry-go-round, but I shook my head. And I refused to have a gypsy read my fortune. I already knew that bad luck was written into the lines on my hands.

The head gardener's house on Mertoun Estate. John Hall's childhood home, 1909-1918

Grandfather had moved to St. Boswells and bought the tobacco shop when he retired from his job as head gardener on nearby Mertoun Estate. My father and his sister Maud and brother George grew up on the estate. They lived in the original manor house, Old Mertoun House, built in 1677, which had become the head gardener's house when a more palatial home was built. Any visit to St. Boswells included a trip out to Mertoun to see the gardens, where we wandered around as if we owned the estate. Our first stop was always the parish church just inside the gates. It wasn't the church that interested us, but the jougs, a metal collar attached by a chain to the wall near the church door. In the olden days the jougs was a form of punishment. The collar was padlocked around an offender's neck to shame him—or her. Peter liked to pretend to be the offender and would fasten the jougs around his neck, while Ann and I took on the role of the virtuous churchgoers and threw insults at him. Our parents wouldn't let us throw clods of dirt, but I'm sure that's what the virtuous churchgoers did long ago.

Another place we loved to visit was Smailholm Tower, an old border keep that is steeped in history. It was a refuge in the time of the border raiders. The Scots would drive their cattle inside while the English raiders hammered at the solid oak door. As a small child, Sir Walter Scott spent a summer with his Aunt Jenny at Sandyknowe Farm next to the tower while recuperating from an illness. Aunt Jenny taught him to read and told him stories of border reivers in her country dialect, stories that echo through Scott's writing.

Our father was a storyteller too, often using Sir Walter's words. We'd stand close together in the dimly lit tower, with shivers down our backs, listening to him recite 'The Eve of St. John."

The Baron of Smaylho'me rose with day,
he spurred his courser on,
without stop or stay, down the rocky way,
that leads to Brotherstone.

The Baron was riding off to confront his wife's lover. While he was gone, his lady continued to meet her knight on lonely Beacon Hill—not knowing that the Baron had killed him and she was meeting his ghost! She entices the ghostly knight to come to the tower on the holy Eve of St. John. By now our father had reached his favorite lines of the poem, where the knight says:

"Who spilleth life, shall forfeit life;
So bid thy lord believe;
That lawless love is guilt above,
This awful sign receive."

He laid his left palm on an ancient beam;
His right upon her hand;
The lady shrunk, and fainting sunk,
For it scorched like a fiery brand.

The sable score of fingers four,
Remains on the board impress'd;
And forever more that lady wore
A covering on her wrist.

As we stood listening to my father's voice, I could feel the ghostly knight right there beside us and looking up I was sure I could see four black imprints on a beam where the knight had placed his fingers.

According to the poem, Smailholm's bold Baron spent the rest of his life as a monk at Melrose tower, while his lady became a nun at Dryburgh Abbey. The Abbey is Sir Walter Scott's final resting place. It lies only a mile from St. Boswells as the crow flies, but seeing we weren't crows, we had to take the longer route over a bridge across the River Tweed when we went to visit Scott's tomb. This took us past Scott's favorite view, a panorama across the Tweed valley toward the Eildon Hills. The horses pulling Sir Walter's carriage became so used to him stopping there to enjoy the view that when they were taking his coffin from his home at Abbotsford to Dryburgh for his burial, they paused to let their master admire his beloved view one last time.

You can't travel far in the border country without running into reminders of Scotland's warring past. In the grounds of Dryburgh Abbey there's a statue honoring King James II. Above his head is a small carving of the cannon that killed him back in 1460, when he was 30. He had been ruling Scotland since he was 6 years old. Being only a little older than that myself, I felt a certain amount of empathy for little James. Ruling all of Scotland was too much responsibility for a 6-year-old. At the time of his death, James was trying to retake Roxburgh Castle. He was sure he'd drive out the English because he had this new weapon. Unfortunately, the cannon misfired.

On the way home from Dryburgh we used to picnic in the shadow of a huge red sandstone statue of William Wallace, one of Scotland's heroes. Back in 1297, he beat Edward I, the Hammer of the Scots, in the Battle of Stirling Bridge. The statue, which is about 30 feet high, was hidden in the trees while weeds and bushes clawed their way over its base. Peter, Ann, and I staged our own battles as we tried to see who could scramble up through the trees onto the base of the statue and be first to grab Wallace's oversized big toe. Meantime our father was busy lighting the primus stove and mother was laying out fish-paste sandwiches so we could all enjoy our afternoon tea.

Smailholm Tower

10

School Days

I was lured into going to school under false pretenses.

A few days before school started my mother took me to meet my teacher, Miss McConnell. I was four years old. I would be in the Wee School, a low white building that was tucked in behind the Big School, a more impressive red sandstone structure. When we entered the classroom, the first thing that caught my eye was a giant rocking horse near the front of the room, next to a window plastered with yellow and red construction-paper tulips. While my mother talked with Miss McConnell, I rode the magnificent horse, galloping through the tulip fields.

I couldn't wait for my first day of school.

But I never got to ride that horse again. It sat there motionless while we all immersed ourselves in the serious business of learning to read. We learned our letters phonetically, all singing out together, *Tapping Tommy says "T"*. A lot of our learning was vocal. As we progressed up through the school, we sang out our times tables in unison, like some sort of Gregorian chant, right up to the twelve-times table. *Twelve times one is twelve. Twelve times two is twenty-four. Twelve times three is thirty-six.* With twelve pennies to the shilling, it was important to know your twelve times table. I suppose that with Britain now on the decimal system, children only learn as far as the ten times table. Which is a pity. The eleven times table has a nice symmetry to it. *Eleven times two is twenty-two. Eleven times three is thirty-three.* And the twelve times table exercises your brain.

Our school days started at nine and ended at four, with an hour break from noon till one, when we went home for lunch—or dinner in those days. We lived over a mile from school, so the dinner break was a rushed affair. Being late back to school wasn't an option. I do remember one occasion when I didn't make it on time. That morning, during a natural history lesson, Miss Richardson threw out a request for someone to bring in frog spawn so we could watch the tadpoles grow into frogs. Being an expert on frog spawn and a child who liked to please her teacher, I saw this as my big chance. I persuaded my friend, Sheila McKay, to come home with me at the dinner break and we'd go to the Baggy Burn to find frog spawn. I knew just where to look.

When we got to my house, I left Sheila sitting beside the stone gatepost. I suppose I didn't ask her to come in because my mother would not have endorsed our frog-spawn scheme. After bolting down my dinner, I found a jam jar, tied a piece of string around its neck to form a handle and smuggled it outside. Sheila and I then headed off to the Baggy Burn, where we eventually found a jellied mass of spawn and transferred it into the jar. As we were trotting up through Henderson's field toward the road, we were startled to hear the distant pealing of the school bell. We broke into a run, with water sloshing out of the jar. When we had almost reached the school, I tripped and the glass jar shattered on the pavement, leaving a sad mess of spawn and broken glass.

We crept into the classroom, looking somewhat dirty and disheveled. Miss Richardson demanded to know why we were late. She wasn't in the least impressed by our explanation. I don't know if she even believed us. After all, we didn't have any frog spawn as evidence. We were sent to stand in the corner – separate corners!

By the time Ann started school I was in Miss Walker's class. We called her Cocky Walker. She didn't make you stand in the corner for any infringement of school rules. She gave you the cane. Peter used to brag about how many times he got the cane in Cocky Walker's class, but I had a different goal. I was going to get through the year without ever suffering the indignity of getting the cane.

I hadn't, however, reckoned on Ann starting school. For the first few weeks our father transported her on his bicycle. He had a second saddle bolted to the crossbar, where Ann perched helmetless, her legs dangling and her hands clutching the handlebar. A few months later, it became my job to make sure she got to school without losing her way or being run over by a bus. Ann wasn't excited about the new arrangement. Neither was I. Ann tended to dawdle and I tended to nag. "Come on Ann! Hurry up, Ann! We're going to be late."

Lockerbie Academy

One afternoon, Ann rebelled and sat down on the curb, refusing to go any farther. I could already feel the sting of that bamboo cane on my outstretched hand for being late for school, but I couldn't just leave her sitting there. I pleaded with her, but Ann remained stubborn. Then I had a sudden inspiration.

"If you get up and walk, I'll tell you a story," I promised.

On that day, Flipperty Gibbet was born.

Flipperty Gibbet was a little Tom-thumb-size character who had a series of chilling adventures. He rode down the gutter on a fallen leaf. Just before he disappeared into the street drain, he was snatched up by a passing crow. When he was about to be dropped into the wide-open mouth of a baby crow in its nest, he wriggled free and fell toward the ground. But before he hit the ground, he landed on a moss-covered branch, where he encountered an angry squirrel . . . The more exciting the story, the faster Ann walked. Over time, I became heartily tired of Flipperty Gibbet, but he did teach me a valuable lesson. If you want to drag your listener—or your reader—along with you, you have to keep your story line moving. Two generations later, Flipperty Gibbet was still doing his job, enticing granddaughter Gillian up the hill on 60th Street after I met her off the school bus.

Thanks to Flipperty, I got through Cocky Walker's class unscathed. Also, I was careful to keep out of trouble. There was a story in our reading book about a frog that fell into a bowl of cream. It began to swim around and around until it finally churned the cream into a lump of butter. By climbing onto the butter, it was able to jump free. We were told to re-tell the story in our own words and say what the moral of the story was. After summarizing the story I wrote:

The moral is that little frogs
Should always stay close-by their bogs.

But just to be on the safe side, I added a more prosaic moral: *Don't give up!* Apparently Miss Walker was amused enough by my couplet that she passed it on to my mother. So from this distance, I realize that Miss Walker probably had a sense of humor, but was a victim of a system that enforced discipline with the cane. She may not have been the witch I remember.

But Mag Watson was a different story. She was a witch with a leather strap. I managed to escape "getting the strap" till halfway through the school year. We'd started to write with pens, dipping the nib into the inkwell in the corner of our desk and carefully forming our cursive letters. One fateful afternoon, when I dipped my pen into the inkwell, the nib caught a little clump of tangled hair in the bottom of the well. The next moment, I was staring with disbelief at a streaky, dark blob of ink on my virgin-white sheet of paper. There was no way of escaping the consequence. I had to line up with the other sloppy writers and get the strap. It didn't sting as much as did the fact that I had spoiled my strap-free record.

By now, the inkwells are gone from the desks, the strap is gone, and probably cursive writing is gone, too. It's too bad about cursive writing.

Lockerbie train station, where Margaret Jean lost her middle name

11

Leading up to War

On the first day of August 1939, I lost my middle name. It happened just before dawn. We were lined up on the platform of the Lockerbie train station with our usual assortment of bags, suitcases, and a steamer trunk. We looked as if we were aiming to cross the Atlantic, but we were just at the start of our annual journey to Mallaig Mhor. While we waited for the train, a fellow traveler struck up a conversation with my mother. She complimented her on her lovely family and how well disciplined we were. In truth, we were standing there quietly because we were only half awake. She then asked our names. "Peter, Margaret Jean, and Ann," my mother answered. The woman looked us over and said, "But there are only three children!" "This one is Margaret Jean," my mother explained, reaching down and playfully pulling at my pigtail.

At that moment, the burden of having two names was suddenly more than I could bear. I had more or less lost my middle name at school because there was never enough room for it at the top of the page, but having someone think that I was two people was the last straw.

I announced that from now on I was going to be Margaret. No more Jean!

We had a long journey ahead of us. We had to change trains in Carstairs, Glasgow, and Fort William. On the last leg, from Fort William to Mallaig, we could look out the window of our compartment up near the engine and see our own tail as the train wound its way around bays and mountains. As we neared the end of the long journey, we watched the sun go down behind the islands of Rhum, Eigg, and Muck. How we loved those names, especially Muck.

By the time we reached Mallaig, by only answering to "Margaret," I had more or less lost my middle name. As we tumbled out of the train the raucous cry of the gulls and the smell of smoke from the kipper factory mingling with the salt sea air told us we were back. And there was Donald MacDonald waiting for us on the dock with his rowboat bobbing in the water. To our mother's relief, the sea was calm. When we rounded the last promontory and saw the little white house waiting for us, we felt that summer had truly arrived.

I think that may have been the year I learned how to swim. Our father would row us out into the bay. Peter and I would jump from the prow of the boat in our heavy woolen bathing suits and dog paddle wildly toward the shore, carried along by

Peter and Ann in swimsuits, circa 1937

the waves and the buoyancy of the salt water. In the course of the summer, I learned to kick like a frog and plough through the water doing breaststroke. And that's how I still swim to this day. I like to see what lies ahead.

Another favorite pastime—one that I'm not proud to recall—was fighting with hermit crabs.

Dozens of buckie shells that had been taken over by hermit crabs scuttled over the floor of the tide pools. We chose our favorites by size or color, then held them close together with the shell openings facing one another, cheering them on as the little crabs reached out clawing the air. The crab that dragged the other one right out of its shell was the winner and got to fight another round.

While we were staging mock battles with hermit crabs or re-enacting Bonnie Prince Charlie evading the English, Europe was heading toward war. Early in August, London had a trial run of the blackout. Later in the month, Parliament passed the Emergency Power Act and military reservists were called up. The following day a treaty of alliance was signed in which Britain promised to defend Poland against any German aggression. With no wireless, we weren't kept abreast of these developments, but I'm sure my parents bought newspapers on their trips to Mallaig. They didn't burden us children with the grim news, though they must have had tense discussions between themselves. One reason for deep concern was that my father was a pacifist, so the prospect of war raised a frightening problem.

On the last day of August, Donald MacDonald rowed us into Mallaig to catch the early train. When we pulled out of the station, we were a bit disconcerted to find we didn't just have the carriage to ourselves; we had the whole train to ourselves. Apparently, all the other holidaymakers had already headed for home. As we traveled farther south, the train did fill up, but there were no women or children. Only young army recruits, many of them already in uniform. And when night fell, the lights didn't come on as we snaked our way through the darkness. That was our first introduction to the blackout and the war hadn't started yet.

It always took a little while for us to get used to being home after those Highland holidays. We'd forgotten how lush and green the border country is compared with the moors and mountains of the north. We waded through the uncut grass on the front lawn and marveled at the height of the broad beans in the vegetable garden. The branches of the apple trees bent under the weight of fruit and we were awed by how dense and leafy the chestnut and copper beech trees had grown. Inside, the house seemed bigger. The air was dank and the closed rooms smelled slightly of gas.

We had barely shaken the sand out of our shoes and unpacked our suitcases when, on September 3rd, Prime Minister Neville Chamberlain gave a short radio address telling an expectant nation that Britain was at war with Germany. I don't remember this momentous announcement. He spoke on Sunday morning at 11:15, so I suppose we were all in church at the time listening to my father preach.

At six o'clock in the evening, King George VI addressed the nation. King George had a stammer and wasn't easy to listen to, but in spite of the hesitancy in his voice, we were all moved by his sincerity as he reached the end of his speech:

"There may be dark days ahead and war may no longer be confined to the battlefield. But we can only do the right as we see the right, and reverently commit our cause to God. If one and all keep resolutely faithful to it, ready for whatever service or sacrifice it may demand, then, with God's help, we will prevail. May He bless and keep us all."

On Monday, when Peter and I headed off to school, my thoughts were focused on the start of a new school year and a new teacher. I knew that Scotland was at war, but Germany was far away. When we reached the High Street, I was surprised to meet up with a group of boys and girls who were all carrying what I took to be Kodak camera cases over their shoulders. It was some time before I realized the boxes they were carrying contained gas masks, not cameras. I immediately began to worry—though not about the war. Would I be in trouble for not bringing my gas mask? If I went home to fetch it, I'd be late, and then I'd be in trouble for sure.

Gas masks had been issued to everyone months earlier and my mother had stuck ours in the linen closet. I'm sure it didn't occur to her to send us to school with them on the second day of the war. Ann, who was only four, had a Mickey Mouse mask with a red rubber face piece. When she turned five, she'd get a gray mask with a pig snout like the rest of us.

For a while, we carried our gas masks to school every day, but that soon fell away. We were, however, required to bring them on the first Monday of each month. That was when we put them on in class to test that they didn't leak by placing a piece of paper the size of an index card over the snout and taking a deep breath. If it was a good seal, the paper stayed in place. The mask smelled funny—of rubber and disinfectant. When you put it on, it was hard not to imagine you could smell gas. We giggled a lot and pretended we weren't worried about poison gas, but I couldn't close my ears to the twisted rumors that floated about. I remember kids whispering that Germans had sprayed poison chemicals on the spider webs that coated the hedges in the autumn. If a strand of web drifted against your face, you'd be scarred for life. It took me a long time to get over my spiderweb phobia.

12

The Phony War

In September 1939, the trains that had been empty at the end of August were suddenly overflowing—not with army recruits, but with children. The First World War, the war that was to end all wars, was fought in the trenches in Europe and the civilian population was mostly spared. This war would be different. Planes from Germany could now fly as far as Britain—planes carrying bombs. These bombs would fall on the women and children in the cities.

Before the war started, the government had worked out an elaborate plan for evacuating school children, pregnant women, and mothers with young children. The entire country was divided into three zones: evacuation, reception, and neutral zones. Children in major cities and in places with heavy industry were in the evacuation zone and would be sent to small towns and rural areas. Lockerbie was a reception zone for children from Glasgow. The billeting officer made a tally of all the empty bedrooms in the town and evacuees were allocated accordingly. Ours was a big, rambling house with several empty rooms. Like most houses in those days, we had only one bathroom.

Peter, Ann, and I awaited our new family members with growing excitement. Peter, of course, was hoping for boys; Ann and I wanted girls. So we were all disappointed when we came home from school one day to find we were sharing our house with a young mother and a screaming 2-year-old. Even though, at the age of 7, cleanliness was not high on my list of priorities, I couldn't help noticing that the little girl was very dirty. She didn't look like she ever went near a bathtub. Maybe sharing our one bathroom wouldn't be a problem.

But sharing one kitchen *was* a problem. My mother and Bunty, the maid, weren't happy. Bunty didn't like washing up the dirty dishes that were abandoned in the sink. She didn't like dealing with the saucepans left on the coal-burning stove. And most of all, she hated the soiled nappies in the laundry hamper.

The young evacuee mother wasn't happy either. She missed the closeness of her neighbors in the Glasgow tenement. She missed having a fish-and-chip shop around the corner where she could buy her fast-food dinner wrapped in newspaper. She missed the sounds of the city. Compared with life back home, Lockerbie was lonely, boring, and quiet. Soon the clouds of discontent grew darker than the clouds of war. When no bombs fell, the mother and her toddler went home. Seeing they had brought next to nothing with them, it wasn't hard for them to pack up and leave.

Soon after this, Edinburgh Gran announced that she and Granddad had decided to come and live with us for the duration of the war. In contrast to the mother and toddler, they arrived with bulging suitcases and hopeful smiles. It wasn't so much the fear of bombs that drove them to move to the country.

It was the iron railings.

Gran's house in Edinburgh had a small patch of grass out front, separated from the street by a fence of wrought-iron railings and a fancy iron gate. With factories hungry for metal to build more Spitfires to fight the enemy, iron railings everywhere became part of the War Effort. Gran thought her house looked naked without its ornamental fence. She hated how people making their way along the street seemed to be walking on her front lawn.

Granddad had his own reasons to complain about the war. Less than a week after the war started, the Football Association suspended all football games, unless organized by the armed forces. Although the ruling was later revised because the sport was considered important to the morale of the country, most of the players on Granddad's beloved Hearts of Midlothian team were conscripted. There wasn't much for the sports editor of the Edinburgh Evening News to write about.

Those early months of the war became known as the Phony War. The dreaded bombs didn't fall from the sky. The air raid sirens only sounded at one o'clock on Saturday afternoons for practice drills. Before too long, like the evacuee mother, Gran and Granddad missed city life. With three children underfoot, their life in Lockerbie probably wasn't lonely and quiet, but after a month or two, they packed their bags and went home.

Early in the summer of 1940, the bombing started in earnest, particularly in the south of England, but Glasgow was also under attack. The frequent air raids resulted in a new wave of evacuees. Because our bedrooms were empty again, we were allocated two girls—Ruth and Rita. They were older than Peter, twelve or thirteen years old. In many ways, they were more worldly wise than we were, but at the same time their ignorance astonished us. They'd never seen a cow. They didn't know that was where milk came from—or maybe they'd just never thought about it. For them, a walk in the countryside held all the unknown terrors of the African bush.

I don't remember how long Ruth and Rita stayed with us. Perhaps their mothers missed them and took them home. Or they may have turned fourteen and were old enough to leave school and find jobs in munitions factories.

Although most of the evacuees came from Glasgow and were accompanied by their teachers, a few came as individuals and were absorbed into our classrooms. Some of them were from English cities in the south and had been sent to stay with relatives in Lockerbie. We were a little suspicious of those English children. In school, we were steeped in Scottish history. Every year our history book began with the Picts and the Scots, and worked its way through warrior heroes like William Wallace and Robert the Bruce. We celebrated our victories and defeats—the Battle of Bannockburn in 1314 and Flodden in 1513. We sang mournful songs: *The Flooers o' the Forest, that focht aye the foremost, the prime o' our land, lie cauld in the clay.* The enemy was always the English. The school year usually ended before the Union of the Crowns in 1603, when King James VI of Scotland became James I of England, uniting the two countries. Now here we were going to school and playing with those descendants of Edward I, the hammer of the Scots!

When they first came, the English evacuees tended to keep together, and we didn't invite them to join in our games of rounders and peavery beds. On at least one occasion we Lockerbie children formed a circle around them in the school playground imitating their accents. Those English children "talked funny." No doubt they thought the same about us. However, by the time skipping season came around, we discovered that we all jumped rope to some of the same jingles.

Christopher Columbus was a mighty man.
He sailed to America in an old tin can.
The can was greasy,
He sailed easy.
Christopher Columbus was a mighty man.

Then one magical day, we discovered that Henderson's field next to Dumfries Road had been converted into a giant play structure. What we were actually seeing were dozens of the tubular metal skeletons that fit onto the backs of army lorries to support the camouflaged canvas covers, but to us it looked like a jungle gym that stretched as far as our eyes could see. As word spread through the town, more and more children gathered. We challenged one another to cross the field without touching the ground, while avoiding kids turning somersaults and playing tag on the metal bars. Broad Glasgow and Lockerbie accents blended with the English voices in the crisp evening air. When it was too dark to see, we made our reluctant way home.

Two days later the field was empty except for a few cows grazing the trampled grass. Each day when Ann and I turned onto Dumfries Road we held our breath, hoping that the metal skeletons had come back. But they never did.

13

Ann's One

The outbreak of war changed everybody's lives. But many changes just crept up on us and, as children, we accepted them. Things like gas masks, the blackout, air raid sirens, and rationing. Four months into the war, in January 1940, food rationing was introduced. Britain relied heavily on imported food, so part of Hitler's strategy was to torpedo supply ships. When food shortages resulted in long queues and soaring prices, rationing came as a welcome answer. We were all issued ration books, color-coded by age. Tan for grown-ups and blue for children from six through sixteen. Ann, who was five, had a green book.

Sugar, bacon, butter, and tea were the first items rationed. They were rationed by weight. Meat rationing followed in March and was rationed by price. Everyone over six years old got one shilling and ten pence worth a week, while Ann with her green book only got eleven pence worth. None of us dreamed back then that Ann would go through all three colors of books before rationing finally ended in 1954.

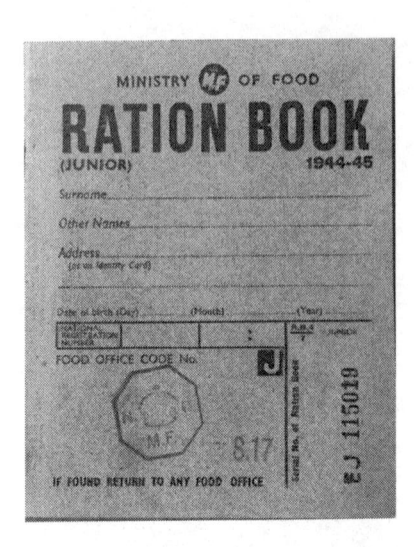

Ration book, identity card, and cookbook

At first, we weren't much affected. My father kept bees, we had a big vegetable garden, and Peter snared the occasional rabbit. We were used to eating what was put before us. And there had not been many exotic items in our diet before the war.

Canned goods and various foods such as dried fruit, breakfast cereal, tapioca, and rice were rationed under a points system. Each person had 16 points a month to spend on these foods any way they wished. The point value for different foods varied from week to week with their availability. I seem to remember that this was announced after the news on Sunday evenings. We didn't pay much attention to the points for rice and tapioca, but we cheered when we heard that points for canned peaches had been reduced—maybe because a shipload had got through from America. Of course, that only meant everyone wanted to use their points on peaches that week and the grocer would run out.

Some of my clearest memories connected with rationing have to do with eggs. We got dried eggs from America in little waxed cardboard boxes with a flag on them. For years I saw the American flag as being dull red, cardboard colored, and blue! Adults could buy one box of dried eggs every eight weeks (equal to a dozen eggs in the shell) whereas children were entitled to two boxes. When you added water to the powder and fried it, it made a little yellow omelet with frilly green edges. I loved those greenish leathery omelets and really missed them after the war.

When the ration for eggs in the shell dropped to less than one egg per person per week, our family decided to go into the chicken business. We outfitted the building in the back yard that had been our museum with nesting boxes and started out with three laying hens. When one went broody we bought twelve fertile eggs from Mr. Aisles' small farm near Eskrigg Pond. Sadly, after four of the eggs hatched, the mother hen lost all interest in the remainder.

So my father, with us three children in tow, headed across the fields to ask Mr. Aisles what had gone wrong. The good farmer kindly offered each of us children a fluffy yellow chick from his incubator. Peter and I wasted no time reaching down into the metal drum and grabbing a chick at random. Ann's arms were too short to reach the chicks, so she pointed to the one she wanted—a sad little creature, standing against the side of the incubator on one leg with its eyes closed. Even Farmer Aisles joined us in trying to dissuade her, but that was the chick Ann had decided on, and she was a child who knew how to get what she wanted. She looked up at her father and asked sweetly, "Do you want me to scream like I usually do?" Before she could utter her first wail, he reached down and handed Ann the poor bedraggled chick. She clutched it tightly in her hand all the way home.

The mother hen accepted her enlarged family. Within a day or two, my chick and Peter's were hard to distinguish from their stepbrothers and sisters as they ventured out into the world. Meanwhile we all shook our heads and worried about Ann's One, still huddling under the mother hen. Ann's One had become its official name. When Peter's chick went through adolescence and grew red feathers, he called it Red. Mine also had red feathers and I named it Jenny, which was a misnomer because Jenny turned out to be a cockerel. One day he disappeared from the flock. I suppose it's possible we had him for dinner, but if we did, he was so disguised that none of us children guessed his fate.

Meantime Ann's One matured into a large white hen with black speckled feathers on her neck. And her personality was as distinctive as her appearance. She didn't identify with the other hens. She preferred to hang out with humans, especially Ann. She often wandered into our house. Perhaps she'd been imprinted during that ride home in Ann's clenched fist.

But it was when she first began to lay that her odd personality really came through. One morning, when my mother went out to bring in the milk, which was delivered to our front door each day, she found a lone cracked egg on the doorstep. The same thing happened the following day, but this time the egg had rolled down the step and lay broken in the driveway. The mystery was solved when my father saw Ann's One squeezing out through a gap in the hen run fence. He did not, however, fix it right away. Instead he placed a nesting box by the front door so that Ann's One could deliver our breakfast egg unbroken along with the morning milk.

14

The Fever Hospital

Beyond the last house on Dumfries Road there once was a small, whitewashed stone, rounded on top and low enough for a child to perch on. It was partly hidden by long grass, but you could still make out the words, *Lockerby, 1 mile* on a metal plate attached to the front of the stone.

"They've spelled Lockerbie wrong," I told my father one summer afternoon when we were on our way to Aisles' farm to buy tomatoes from his greenhouse. "Lockerbie ends in *i-e* not *y*."

"That's the old spelling," my father answered. "This stone is a little bit of history."

The conversation took place before September 1939. I can be sure of that because after Hitler invaded Poland the metal plate was pried off the milestone to become part of the War Effort. Behind the removal of the metal plate was a more sinister reason. A decree had gone out all over Britain, even to our remote town in southwest Scotland, that any signposts that might provide invading German soldiers with a clue as to where they were had to be taken down. The idea of enemy soldiers dropping from the sky in parachutes was the stuff of nightmares. That they wouldn't know which way to go was of little comfort. They might turn up at our back door.

Like tramps.

Times were hard in the late thirties, with lots of people out of work. Some of them wandered from town to town looking for odd jobs or a hand out. These tramps often turned up at the manse door and my mother would give them a *jelly piece*—that's a slice of bread and jam—or a few pennies, hoping they would be on their way. On one occasion, when my father wasn't home, an unsavory-looking, unshaved stranger knocked on the door and my mother herded us children into the broom closet under the stairs where we all hid until the man gave up knocking and went on his way.

Once the war started, I didn't have to worry about tramps any more. If they didn't join the army, they could find jobs in munitions factories. And pretty soon I stopped worrying about bombs and German soldiers. It was easy to tell myself that the war was far away and would soon be over. Practice air-raid drills at school became no more alarming than fire drills. When the warning siren sounded, we all marched out to the edge of the playground and lined up inside the dark cycle shed that had been barricaded with sandbags. The tin roof wouldn't have saved us from a direct hit. The sandbags were there to protect us from shrapnel and flying glass. After a month or two the bags began to leak, sometimes helped by poking fingers. Rivulets of sand ran down and turned the edge of the tarmac into a giant sandbox where the primary children drew designs and mazes in the sand.

Our main source of news was the wireless. Every evening, at six o'clock, my parents would tune in and listen with somber faces as a disembodied voice declared, "This is the BBC news with Frank Philips reading it." We were supposed to learn to recognize the announcers' voices so we wouldn't be fooled if the Germans took over the broadcasting system and filled us with false information. However, I didn't pay much attention. But in May, 1940, it became harder to ignore the news, when Germany invaded France, Belgium, and Holland. British troops trapped on the continent had to retreat and were rescued from the port of Dunkirk by a heroic fleet of ships that included everything from Navy destroyers to private yachts and fishing boats. Winston Churchill, who had just replaced Neville Chamberlain as Prime Minister, warned us that we shouldn't look on the rescue of the troops as a victory. "Wars are not won by evacuation," he told us in his gravelly voice.

After France fell, the possibility that Britain might be invaded next became real. When wailing sirens interrupted our sleep, we tumbled out of our beds and headed for our air-raid shelter—that same broom closet under the stairs where we'd hidden from the tramp. We crouched in the spidery darkness, shivering in our nightgowns and pajamas, waiting for the wail of the All Clear siren. Once again,

I worried about bombs and German soldiers dropping out of the sky. The warnings usually happened twice a night. Lockerbie lay in the flight path between Germany and its main target, the Glasgow docks. First we'd hear the siren as the planes approached from the south, and then the All Clear when they were out of range. This was repeated when the planes made their return journey.

At some point we gave up on the broom closet and stayed in our beds—until the bombs fell on the border village of Eaglesfield. A group of people attending a church meeting decided to head for home at the sound of the wailing siren and rushed out of the church hall. Light spilling from the open doorway must have caught the attention of a pilot in a plane overhead. One of the stream of bombs was a direct hit. Five people were killed. That weekend some children from school cycled over to see the crater. Mother wouldn't let Peter and me go, but for a long time my dreams were haunted by a deep hole full of broken bodies. And after that, we took the warning sirens seriously and were very careful about the blackout. We'd learned that if the German planes didn't unload all their bombs in their targets to the north, they had to get rid of them before landing back in Germany. Anywhere could be a target.

That same summer Ann came down with scarlet fever. The rest of the family was quarantined for three weeks and Ann was whisked off in an ambulance to Lochmaben Hospital four miles away. Because it was summer and school was out, the quarantine didn't affect me much, but I was bored without Ann's company.

Lochmaben Hospital

Before Ann left, Mother gave her a sweet little doll in a yellow knitted dress with knickers to match. I don't know why Mother had a brand new doll stowed away in a cupboard. Maybe she'd rescued it from the church ladies. Some time earlier, the ladies in the Women's Guild had bought a box of naked dolls with the idea of making clothes for them and selling them at a profit at their annual Sale of Work, but one of the women noticed *Made in Germany* printed on the dolls' backs. She urged the other women to smash the dolls. It wasn't patriotic for British children to play with toys made by the enemy.

So although I missed Ann while she was in hospital, some of my impatience for her to come home was because I was looking forward to introducing the doll in the yellow dress to our doll family. When we played school with our dolls, she'd be the new evacuee who'd been sent to live in the country to escape the bombs in the city. To my great disappointment, when Ann came home after five weeks, she didn't bring the doll in the yellow dress with her. It had to stay in quarantine in Lochmaben Hospital where the sick children could play with it.

One frosty morning in early December of that same year, I stumbled downstairs in my nightgown complaining about a sore throat. My mother placed a cool hand on my forehead and then told me to stick out my tongue. She didn't need to wait for Dr. McLaughlin to tell her that I'd come down with scarlet fever. She'd seen that "white strawberry tongue" before. She sent me back upstairs to bed.

In spite of the sore throat, I felt a thread of excitement on hearing the words *scarlet fever*. It was now my turn to be the important one. I'd finally get to play with the doll with the yellow dress. And I'd get to play with all the other left-behind dolls.

A little while later, Mother brought me a cup of hot milk and toast fingers served on the special china we only got to use when we were sick. But I wasn't hungry. Then Dr. McLaughlin showed up, wearing his long black coat and carrying his little black bag. He took my temperature, examined my rash, and told me to stick out my tongue. Yes, I did indeed have scarlet fever, he announced solemnly. Then he went on to say that all the beds in Lochmaben Hospital were full, so I'd have to go to the hospital in Annan, 10 miles away. I didn't mind. It meant I'd get a longer ride in the ambulance. I could count the number of times on one hand I'd been in a car. Though I felt a bit sad that I wouldn't get to play with the doll with the yellow dress. When I reminded my mother that Ann got a doll when *she* went to the hospital, Mother dismissed the notion, saying I was a big girl. I was eight years old.

I'd imagined the hospital would be a big square room full of left-behind toys, but it wasn't like that at all. It was a long, narrow ward with a double row of identical metal beds. My bed was half way down the ward. As darkness fell—and it falls early in December in Scotland—the nurses closed the blackout curtains. When the supper cart came around, I had no appetite for the jam sandwich, but I managed to drink a little hot sweet tea.

When bedtime arrived and the lights were dimmed, I missed the nightly ritual of Mother tucking us in, saying, *Good night, sleep tight, and don't let the bed bugs bite!* Ann and I would chant back: *If they do, take your shoe, and hit them till they're black and blue!* Lying there in that long bare ward full of sniffling, snoring strangers, I felt lonely not having Ann's bed next to mine.

Not long after I fell into an uneasy sleep, I was wakened by the wail of an air raid siren. Then I heard the sound of footsteps coming down the length of the ward. In the dim light, I could make out the night nurse with her starched cap. She stopped at each bed. After examining the clipboard attached to the railing at the foot of the bed, she motioned to the patient to get up and follow the other women and girls down the hall. But when she came to my bed, she took a quick glance at my chart and passed me by.

The nurse didn't stop to explain that newly admitted patients with a high fever were deemed better off staying in bed than risking coming down with pneumonia by going down to the drafty underground shelter. She may have thought I was asleep. All I knew was that I was left there, trembling and alone, in that shadowy ward, which seemed to have grown longer—a dark tunnel with empty metal beds lined up as far as I could see.

Then I heard the throbbing drone of the German planes, planes heavy with bombs. They sounded completely different from the British planes we heard in the daytime. I held my breath, praying that the blackout was intact. Eaglesfield village where the bombs had fallen was close to Annan.

After a while the All Clear sounded. The planes were on their way to bomb the dockyards in Glasgow. But they would soon be back and the sirens would wail again. I lay awake waiting.

I suppose there were other air raids while I was in the hospital and I must have graduated to being allowed to go to the shelter, but I have no memory of that. All I remember is that the days dragged on just like the war. We were always hearing that some day the war would be over, but we never seemed to get there. It was the same way with those five long weeks in the hospital.

When Ann was in hospital, my parents visited her each week. Lochmaben was only four miles away and was within easy cycling range. When I was in hospital, because they had no car, they asked a friend to use some of his meager petrol ration to bring them over from Lockerbie. It wasn't a great visit. I stood on my bed and shouted to them through the high window. When I complained about having mince and potatoes for dinner every single day, they shushed me. I didn't really mind mince and potatoes, but I'd heard other people complaining about the food to their visitors and it was hard to think of anything to say through a closed window. When it was time for them to leave, I began to cry. A nurse told me I was too old to cry and that only made me cry all the more. That was the only time they came. Perhaps they figured their visit upset me. Or they may have been heeding the signs that were posted everywhere, asking IS YOUR JOURNEY REALLY NECESSARY? I recalled how they had cycled over to see Ann, but in all fairness, the twenty-mile round trip to Annan would have been hard work on those heavy, single-geared bikes that they walked up all the hills.

My birthday is on Christmas Eve, so I spent my ninth birthday and Christmas day in hospital. Back then, Christmas wasn't a big holiday in Scotland, but we always hung up stockings and had presents and a tree with wax candles. In the hospital, each child received one present. Mine was a box of plasticine (modeling clay). Doreen in the next bed got a set of doll's dishes. We spent a happy day making food out of my plasticine and serving it on her miniature dishes—bananas and oranges and grapes, all the things we remembered from before the war. That evening, the nurse scolded me for staining my sheet with the plasticine and said she'd take it away if it happened again. After that, Doreen and I played on the cold floor between our beds, but my dirty sheet was left unwashed. Soap was in short supply.

A few days before I was due to go home, the nurse brought me my clothes. "Oh, dear! Your mother didn't send your shoes, only your bedroom slippers," she said. Then holding up a boy's undershirt, she exclaimed, "And look at this—she sent your brother's winter vest!" I felt humiliated. It *was* my brother's undershirt, or vest as we called it. But it was no mistake. It was what I wore in the winter, even before the war—a boy's nasty, scratchy, hand-me-down winter vest. I didn't contradict the nurse and left her to think my mother must have sent it by mistake.

Ann claims that before she was released from the hospital she was doused with disinfectant. I don't remember that happening. But I do know that after I was sent home I developed rheumatism in my ankles. Mother blamed it on the nurses who had, a few days before I was released, sent me outside in the snow in my bedroom slippers. We were all great believers in fresh air, but Mother was furious that it came at the expense of cold, wet feet.

When I was finally well enough to go back to school, the doctor suggested I attend half-days for the first week. During that week when I only went to school in the morning and came home at noon with my leather school bag on my back, my classmates kept asking why I was taking my school bag home when it wasn't the end of the day. I replied loftily that the doctor said I only had to go to school for half a day. I had that same conversation on the Friday morning. But when I got home, Mother told me she figured I was now well enough to go school for the whole day. Maybe she had something planned for the afternoon. She refused to listen when I explained that I couldn't go back because I'd told everyone I only had to go to school in the morning. No one else would be carrying a school bag at that time of day. I'd be conspicuous . . . humiliated. But Mother insisted. So I dragged myself back to school, feeling totally misunderstood. Life back home wasn't perfect after all.

15

The House Next Door

The houses on Dumfries Road, like most houses in Lockerbie, had names not numbers. Brooklands was a solid sandstone building similar to ours with a spacious garden front and back. It belonged to Mr. Caruthers. Peter, Ann, and I only knew the old man as a pale face that occasionally appeared at an upstairs window. He never went outside. No one tended the garden and the uncut lawn grew as wild as a hay field. We sometimes sneaked across the lawn and out through Mr. Caruthers' garden gate, leaving a trail like a rabbit run through the long grass. We called it our short cut even though it involved squeezing through the rhododendron bushes that edged our driveway and scrambling through the dividing hedge. Sometimes we saw Mr. Caruthers peering out his window. He would raise his shaky old hand, but whether it was a wave or an admonishing finger we couldn't tell.

When Mr. Caruthers finally did make a trip outside, it was in a hearse. We watched him go from our own upstairs window. For a while, the disquieting thought that the old man might be keeping an eye on his property from up in heaven

Brooklands, the house next door, circa 1970

made us wary of using the short cut. But then the army requisitioned Brooklands to house officers from the army camp farther down the road. The groups of soldiers that came and went were no keener on gardening than Mr. Caruthers had been. The bushes grew bushier and the grass longer.

The soldiers were congenial neighbors. On several occasions they came over to solicit cooking advice from my mother. They also borrowed pots and pans and cookbooks. When the pots were returned, they were often burned black, which was a nuisance because you couldn't replace them during the war. Metal was in high demand for the War Effort and factories weren't making kitchenware. The soldiers, however, did repay us with little kindnesses. I still remember the two huge gallon jars of plum jam. Due to the shortage of fruit, my mother had tried a recipe for making jam out of turnips. It wasn't a big hit. Even so, we were ready to try turnip jam again when those big jars of plum jam were empty.

Peter, Ann, and I spent a lot of time spying on the soldiers. They came and went in big army lorries, which barely fitted between the two columnar sandstone gateposts at the end of the driveway. A round stone ball topped each post, though soon only one post was topped by a ball and the other post leaned at an awkward angle. To make the driveway entrance easier to navigate, someone coated the posts with fluorescent white paint. I worried that this might make them visible from the sky. Also, the soldiers weren't as careful about the blackout as we were. They didn't have to be because the air raid wardens didn't enforce fines on soldiers. I didn't think our good habits would protect us from a stray bomb if German planes spotted the lights next door.

With the arrival of the soldiers, Brooklands presented a new challenge. Trespassing through the neglected garden was no longer enough—we wanted to see inside the house. One Saturday morning, from our hiding place in the rhododendron bushes, we watched a group of soldiers pack up and leave. They took everything with them, including, according to my mother, one of her cookbooks. Now was our chance!

After the last lorry pulled out of the driveway, the three of us walked boldly up to the front door. To our dismay, it was locked, and so was the back door. We tried all the downstairs windows, Ann and I going around the house in one direction, Peter in the other. We were almost all the way around, when we heard Peter calling to us, his voice strangely muffled.

"In here," he shouted.

He'd found his way in through a small square hatch, which opened into the coal cellar. At the other side of the cellar was an unlocked door leading into the house. I helped Ann climb through the hatch and then followed her across the dark cellar, bits of coal crunching under our feet. We came out into a hallway that led to the kitchen and the pantry. There was also a back stairway up to what had been the maids' rooms. We pushed through a swing door that opened into the front hall where there was a grander stairway. Peter was already on his way up to the main bedrooms. We followed him, our footsteps echoing on the uncarpeted stairs. The whole place smelled of cigarette smoke and boiled cabbage. The bedrooms were unfurnished except for the occasional wardrobe or chest of drawers. You could tell where pictures had once hung by dark rectangles on the faded wallpaper.

We moved over to the bay window, where we had an aerial view of our shortcut. We also had a view of something more unsettling—an army lorry swinging into the driveway, barely missing the white gateposts.

"Run!" Peter yelled. "It's more soldiers. Take the back stairs."

Ann clattered after him, but I just stood there "rooted to the spot with fear" as they always said in books. Now I could see soldiers spilling out of the lorry, heading for the front door. Soldiers with rifles. Soldiers who might shoot first and ask questions afterwards. Maybe they were enemy soldiers, Germans who had dropped out of the sky . . .

That thought was enough to make me turn and run after the others, down the back stairs, and through the door that opened into the coal cellar. When I scrambled out the hatch I saw Ann and Peter waiting for me, crouched under the bushes. A few minutes later we were safe on our side of the hedge.

We were never tempted to go inside the house next door again. There was nothing to see in those bare, empty rooms.

But there was another house farther down Dumfries Road that fascinated me. Clairmont House belonged to R.Y. McKay, the lawyer. He had a peach tree growing in a greenhouse behind the house and he once presented our family with a ripe peach. My mother divided it into five equal pieces and we each got to taste that sweet, juicy fruit. It tasted so good, I found myself wishing I were an only child. That way the peach would only have had to be divided into three.

But it wasn't the peach tree in the greenhouse that made Clairmont special. It was the turret room on the southeast corner of the house. There may have been a Mrs. McKay. I don't remember. But I do know that there were no children. All the same, in my imagination, I furnished the small circular room with child-size furniture and filled it with toys. A window seat with dark red velvet cushions followed the contour of the wall. The fireplace was decorated with blue and white Dutch tiles, and on the mantelpiece above it were two toy soldiers standing in sentry boxes. A child's desk and a small chair stood near the door. Against the opposite wall was a cupboard with doors slightly ajar revealing books and dolls, and there was a small table set for tea.

Clairmont House. Photo by Lenna Tiryaki

Each time I walked past Clairmont House, I wished that someone would come running down the driveway and invite me to come in and play with the toys in the magical turret room, but of course it never happened.

However, many years later, I again visited the turret room in my imagination. It was while writing

Searching for Shona, a story about two evacuees who trade destinations and take on one another's identity. One of the girls goes into a house that has just been vacated by soldiers. But this time it isn't Brooklands. Instead it's Clairmont House. She finds her way up the long spiral staircase to the tower room and there it is, just the way I always wanted it to be. The window seat with the red velvet cushions. The fireplace with the blue Dutch tiles. The toy soldiers on the mantelpiece. And dolls spilling out of the cupboard.

16

The War Effort

Supporting the War Effort kept everyone busy.

My father was always attending some meeting or other. The ministers of the other two churches in Lockerbie had signed on to be army chaplains, leaving my father in charge of the three Presbyterian churches. Sunday services were held in each of the churches in turn. With three congregations and soldiers from the neighboring army camp all praying to win the war, both the morning and evening services were crowded. Now the singing drowned out the organ, especially when we sang *Onward Christian soldiers, marching as to war.*

My mother worked in the canteen next to the railway station preparing sandwiches and urns of tea for soldiers from the nearby training camp and for soldiers passing through on their way to the front. She rolled bandages and made dressings for wounds using sphagnum moss. In addition, she had lots to keep her busy at home after Bunty, our maid, went to work in a factory to do her part for the war effort.

Because so many farm workers were off fighting the war, people worried that the potatoes might rot in the fields. Starting in 1941, the school summer holiday was shortened to three weeks and we were given three weeks of Potato Holidays in October so that children could bring in the harvest. Even though Peter assured us that it wasn't fun scrabbling in the cold dirt looking for potatoes, Ann and I were jealous. We were too young to help—or maybe our mother wouldn't let us. Washing Peter's muddy clothes every night was as much as she could manage.

Although Ann and I didn't get to dig potatoes to help feed a hungry nation, we did contribute to the health of the nation by gathering rose hips from the hedgerows along Dumfries Road. Concerned about the lack of Vitamin C in young people's diets, the government introduced the Vitamin Welfare Scheme in 1941, providing blackcurrant juice and rose hip syrup free for children under two. Cod liver oil for Vitamin D wasn't so popular. I think Ann and I were paid for our rose hips, but we never got rich.

My most memorable opportunity to be part of the War Effort was through a school project. One afternoon, all the children in Primary 4 were marched up to the sewing room in the Big School, which was what we called the Secondary School. Miss Johnston, the sewing teacher, greeted us from behind a wall of wool—khaki and air-force blue.

"We're going to do our part to win the war," she told us proudly. "We're going to knit scarves and balaclava helmets, and squares that we'll stitch together for blankets."

"What if you can't knit?" one of the boys asked.

"Knitting's sissy," someone else muttered.

"If women can work in factories, boys can learn to knit," Miss Johnston said sternly. "Those of you who are new to knitting can make squares. And I don't want any dropped stitches. It would be a terrible thing if some poor young man at the battle front caught pneumonia because he had a hole in his blanket where one of you had carelessly dropped a stitch."

I could see that knitting for the armed forces was going to be a big responsibility. Even so, I quickly decided I wasn't going to knit boring squares or a boring scarf. I was going to knit a balaclava helmet. For an airman. I preferred the blue wool.

We all lined up to get yarn and instructions.

"What pattern?" Miss Johnston asked.

"The balaclava helmet, please," I said.

"Can you turn a heel?"

"I thought it was a hat, Miss," I said, puzzled.

"It is—but it's like knitting a sock without a toe."

"I can do that," I assured her, and smiled confidently. I'd been knitting clothes for my dolls since I was 4 years old. Knitting was something we did in the long winter evenings, sitting close to the fire. In those days we had no television to distract us.

We girls were all impatient to get started on our projects, but first we had to teach the boys to knit.

"It's easy," we kept telling them in superior voices. "In, over, through, off. In over, through, off."

Those boys were really slow.

Meantime Miss Johnston kept reminding us what important work we were doing. She read us a poem about a girl working in a factory that had a beat to it that made the knitting go faster.

She's the girl that makes the thing
that drills the hole that holds the spring
That drives the rod that turns the knob
that works the thing-ummy-bob.
She's the girl that makes the thing
that holds the oil that oils the ring
That takes the shank that moves the crank
that works the thing-ummy-bob.

The poem went on for several more verses.

When Miss Johnston reached the end, she looked pink-cheeked and damp-eyed. Then she smiled and told us that like the girl who makes the ring that drills the hole that holds the spring, our squares and scarves and helmets were helping to win the war.

We girls all took our knitting seriously. We arrived at school early and sat knitting on the front steps waiting for the door to be opened. We knitted our way through playtime and lunchtime.

No more skipping and rounders. I even knitted as I walked home with Ann beside me carrying the ball of wool.

And every time I knitted a stitch, I pulled the wool tight, not wanting to leave any space between the stitches for the wind to whistle through and give my airman pneumonia. It slowed me down, pulling on every stitch, but eventually I turned the heel. The helmet was taking shape.

"What is it?" Peter asked one evening.

"A balaclava helmet," I answered through clenched teeth as I pulled the wool tight.

"A what?"

"A balaclava helmet."

"For a doll?" Peter asked.

"Of course not," I said. "It's for an airman. It's my War Effort."

"They don't have airmen with heads that small," Peter pointed out.

For the first time, I stopped and looked critically at the balaclava helmet. What Peter said was true. It was a very small helmet. I tried to stretch it, but I'd pulled every stitch so tight there was no give at all.

"I followed the pattern," I wailed. "I cast on the right number of stitches."

"The tension's wrong," my mother said, taking a look at the knitting.

"What's tension?"

"You've pulled the stitches too tight. I'm afraid you'll have to start over. I'll help you," she offered.

I tearfully unraveled the whole thing and started over. Now I knew why they called it the War EFFORT.

The balaclava helmet wasn't my worst knitting experience. The incident of the gym shorts was far more humiliating. And this time my mother was to blame.

I knew she wasn't going to be happy when I told her I needed black gym shorts for school. Clothing coupons had been introduced a year earlier, but because factories were so busy making uniforms for the armed forces, the clothing ration had just been farther reduced. She'd complain that we didn't have enough coupons to buy shorts that would only be worn one period a day when we all needed new shoes.

However, she greeted my request quite cheerfully. "I have some black wool in the trunk upstairs," she said. "I can easily knit you some shorts."

I groaned. I could already see those clinging woolen shorts.

"The teacher said we could make them from blackout material," I suggested.

"With so many windows, we've used up our blackout material," my mother answered. "I'll start knitting tonight."

In gym class, the following Monday, the girls turned up in a variety of shorts, but no one else was wearing knitted ones. I was a fairly sturdy child and the shorts were not flattering. However, no one commented on them. We had gym with the girls in the class above us and there was someone I really liked, though she rarely noticed me—Nicky Wilson. She was wearing very sporty navy shorts, obviously not homemade from blackout material. When it was time for relay races, Nicky, who was one of the captains, chose me to be on her team. She chose me near the middle, not at the end like a leftover. Maybe my knitted shorts didn't look so terrible after all.

I wasn't the fastest runner in the class, but that day I felt as if I could fly. The first race involved jumping through a wooden hoop, picking up a beanbag, and bringing it back to the next girl in line. When it was my turn, I exploded into action, raced down the gym, jumped through the hoop—and was stopped dead in my tracks. A small nail that held the wooden hoop together caught a stitch in the despicable woolen shorts. When I tried to pull free, the stitch grew longer and the shorts tighter. The girls on the other team continued to run and jump and pass beanbags while I remained ensnared by the nail for an eternity of time.

When I went home and told my mother about my humiliating experience, she didn't seem to understand. She just told me that we all had to make do because there was a war on. A war on! Grownups were forever reminding us that there was a war on. "Eat your cabbage. Don't you know there's a war on?" "No, you can't have money for the picture show—there's a war on!" It never had anything to do with the argument.

Yes, I knew there was a war on. And I was a casualty.

17

Turning Points

Although America's entry into the war after Pearl Harbor raised everyone's spirits, Japan's conquests in the Pacific resulted in stricter rationing of rice, tea, and sugar. Ann and I weren't worried by smaller helpings of rice pudding or weaker tea, but making an eight-ounce bar of chocolate last for a month was hard. The sweetie ration was raised to twelve ounces later that year, though that wasn't much to rejoice over.

The winter of 1942 was unusually cold. With the shortage of coal, this should have been an added misery, but in Lockerbie everyone looked forward to a deep freeze. When Eskrigg Pond froze over, the old men gathered up curling stones that had been acting as doorstops and, war or no war, headed for the ice. Shops and businesses closed early, and some shops didn't bother to open at all.

I can still hear the ring of the stones and the voices of the curlers calling *Sweep, sweep, sweep,* as we made our careful way along the slippery wooden walkway that led out to a duck blind, where we sat down to put on our skates, fiddling with the keys as we tightened the skates onto our shoes. Peter soared off to join a group of boys playing a makeshift game of hockey, being careful to stay clear of the curlers, while Ann and I wobbled our way onto the ice. In my memory the moon was always full, reflecting a path across the black ice.

When a heavy snowfall put an end to curling, the old men were grumpy, but we just exchanged our skates for our sledges and headed for the slope in Henderson's field. After the snow melted we were back in our dark world. For a while there was a craze for wearing little round phosphorescent badges when we went out at night, so we didn't bump into one another in the dark.

The other big event of 1942 was that it was the year I sat the "Qualifying Exam." This was a test you took when you were eleven that decided your whole future. If you did well, you entered the "A" stream in Secondary school and learned Latin and French, eventually qualifying you to go to a University. I was a bookish child and wasn't worried about the exam. I was quick at what we called "mental arithmetic." I didn't panic at questions such as: *How much change do you get out of half-a-crown when you buy a gallon of milk at a penny ha'penny a pint?* The test, which has been replaced by the "Eleven Plus", must have become easier in the early '70s when Britain adopted the decimal system for their money.

Most children, including Peter, continued at Lockerbie Academy for another three years after taking the Qualifying Exam. Those who didn't leave school at fourteen could transfer to Dumfries Academy for the final three years of their Secondary education. My parents decided to send me to Dumfries Academy for all six years of Secondary School, so I started there at the same time as Peter. I don't think I had any say in this decision, but it meant that Ann and I now had separate lives and friends. No more walking to school together.

Dumfries is twelve miles from Lockerbie. Peter and I caught a bus that ran right past our house. At eight o'clock in the morning, we would stand on the verge of the road with wavering flashlights to hail the double-decker bus, a dark, looming shadow with its headlights pointed down to the road so that it was invisible from the air. Peter always scooted upstairs to sit with his rowdy classmates, while I crept into the lower deck and sat among the daily commuters. In the winter, the journeys to and from school were made in the dark.

Dumfries Academy was a school with a long tradition—a *really* long tradition. Although I don't ever remember learning this while I was a student, the school was founded in 1330 and is one of the oldest state schools in Scotland. When

Dumfries Academy, Primary School

Dumfries Academy, Secondary School

I arrived there that first morning, not knowing anyone, we were herded into the assembly hall where we would gather each morning for Prayers and Announcements. We were all dressed alike in our school uniforms. The girls wore gym tunics, white blouses, striped ties, and maroon blazers emblazoned with the school crest and motto—*Doctrina Promovet*. As I stood there nervously looking around, I worried that I might never be able to tell all those uniformed girls apart.

Clothes rationing had come into effect the year before I started Dumfries Academy and lasted until 1949, the year I started University. Outfitting me with my school uniform took about a third of my annual allocation of clothing coupons, but because I spent more than a third of my life wearing my uniform, it wasn't an issue. What bothered me more was that I had a utility blazer. Most children did, but I envied the ones who had inherited pre-war blazers from older siblings. They were softer and fuzzier.

Utility clothing, which was marked by a symbol that resembles two little Pac-Man characters, had been introduced in 1941. The huge need for uniforms for the armed forces and the scarcity of raw materials had resulted in a shortage of clothes for civilians. To increase efficiency and to keep prices down, clothing factories were restricted to using a limited range of fabrics and designs. Women turned out to be more accepting of utility clothes than men, who grumbled about short socks and no turn-ups on their trousers. They especially disliked having fewer pockets.

On that first day of school I was assigned to class 1A, and continued through the school with most of those same classmates. My closest friend, Eleanor Dobie, lived in Dumfries. I sometimes spent weekends with her. I must have been a very unsatisfactory houseguest because all I wanted to do was read her copy of *Gone with the Wind*. We worked our way through it, reading parts of it aloud to one another. We paid more attention to the American Civil War than the war we were actually engaged in. And then there were the Gallic Wars to worry about in our Latin class, where our Latin teacher, Mr. Smith, was our adversary. He hurled pieces of chalk at students who were slow to answer. Luckily, his aim was poor.

In our history class we had finally united the crowns of Scotland and England in 1603 and their parliaments in 1707, though in both cases I felt a bit of a grievance. With the union of the Crowns, King James VI, who had ruled Scotland since he was 13 months old, had to move to London and become James I. Uniting the parliaments also involved moving to London.

We were constantly tested on significant dates in history. The teacher would name an event, such as the Battle of Waterloo, and we had to say what happened and when. I enjoyed this Trivial Pursuit approach to history until the day I was faced with the Battle of El Alamein. Nothing jumped into my mind, though there was a ring of familiarity about the name. I tentatively suggested it had been a turning point during the Third Crusade. Most significant events were turning points. "That would make it the thirteenth century," I added, sounding more confident.

The teacher gave a howl of derision. "Don't you listen to the news?" she asked. "Don't you realize you are living though history?"

Class picture, 1943. Margaret is in the front row.

She went on to inform me that I was seven centuries out, and that General Montgomery's victory at the Battle of El Alamein had turned the tide in the North African campaign. So at least I was right about it being a turning point! And although I made a resolution to listen to the news on the wireless, I soon began to shut the war out again. My mind was mostly focused on homework and friends.

One of my happiest memories of those school years is camping trips to Betty Chapman's sheep farm in the hills near Dunscore village. The core group of campers included Betty, Eleanor, Isobel Bowman, and myself. Sometimes other brave souls joined us. We called ourselves the PCL—the Private Camper's League. Eleanor, who was a Girl Guide, was our chief organizer. She had been camping with her guide troop and knew how to cook on a primus stove and make dampers on an open fire. Dampers consisted of thick dough that you wrapped around a stick and toasted like a marshmallow. Transporting our equipment to the farm was difficult because this was before lightweight materials. Our tent was of heavy canvas and our bedrolls were made from bulky woolen blankets. We looked as if we were setting off to conquer the North Pole.

It was on one of those camping trips that I discovered peanut butter—though I didn't actually taste it. Eleanor's parents had received a care package from the United States and her mother generously added a jar of peanut butter to our food supplies. When we opened it, we were repelled by the thick layer of oil on top, so we drained it off. Then we found we didn't have a strong enough knife to dig out what was left in the jar. How on earth did Americans spread this stuff on bread? We ditched the peanut butter and contented ourselves with a jelly piece.

Royal family on VE Day

18

Victory

The year was 1945. May 8th, 1945. The war was over. Hitler was dead and the Germans defeated.

Victory in Europe Day was greeted with dancing in the streets, parades, and bonfires on hilltops. London, which had suffered the most, celebrated the most exuberantly. Revelers filled the streets. King George VI and Queen Elizabeth stepped out onto their balcony at Buckingham Palace no less than eight times to greet their excited subjects, while Princess Elizabeth and Princess Margaret mingled with the happy crowds below. Churchill gave a short speech telling the rejoicing people, "This is your victory!"

Even before victory was officially announced, the government, which had done such a thorough job of seeing that everything was fair and equitable during the war, was still taking care of us like an overanxious parent. The Board of Trade promised that, until the end of May, we could buy cotton bunting without coupons to make banners and rosettes, as long as the cotton was red, white, or blue. The Home Office told us we could have bonfires, but we were only to use material of no salvage value. I don't know if the material in the bonfires on hilltops in Dumfriesshire had no salvage value, but when the fires lit up the night sky it was wonderful not to have to worry about the blackout.

Parade celebrating VE Day, 1946. Ann is third from the right.

For almost six years we'd been looking forward to "Life after the War," a golden time of freedom and plenty. Of course, it didn't turn out that way. Soldiers returned to an uncertain civilian life. Many of them didn't come home. The end of rationing was nowhere in sight. In fact, a year after the war ended, bread was rationed for the first time. It was harder to be upbeat about restrictions that resulted from a wet summer ruining the wheat crop than when it was about winning a war.

It wasn't until the war was over that we began to hear the full extent of the horrors of the

Nazi regime. When the news reels at the picture houses morphed from showing the happy faces of Londoners celebrating victory to emaciated bodies in the concentration camps, I shut out the news again. I scarcely noticed when Japan was finally defeated in August, with the mushroom cloud over Hiroshima casting a sobering shadow of what future wars might bring.

Some of our peacetime disappointments were minor. When we got our first post-war banana, cousin Ian, who didn't remember what a banana tasted like, bit into his with high expectations. Then his face crumpled and he began to cry. He didn't like the mushy taste. We offered to eat his banana for him, but he shook his head vigorously. He'd waited six years for this moment and he wasn't going to let anyone else enjoy it.

Lockerbie, which had been a receiving zone for evacuees at the beginning of the war, was now a receiving zone again, but this time there was no billeting officer. Families could sign up to host near-starved children from European countries that had been occupied by the Nazis. Taking in a child was strictly voluntary. We signed up and were assigned a little Dutch boy called Jan. Jan was a quiet boy. Quiet to the point that he didn't speak at all. Of course he didn't know English and we didn't speak Dutch, but even when Ann took him to school he didn't talk to the other Dutch children who were staying in Lockerbie.

We had a small-scale billiard table in the playroom and that was where Jan spent all his time. He played with fierce concentration and didn't seem to want anyone to join him. He spent hours playing by himself. Maybe he was homesick, but he didn't seem unhappy. He was just quiet. So we fed him and Ann took him to school. When the children returned to Holland, we missed the strange little quiet boy who had lived in the playroom. I don't think he missed us, but I'm sure he would have liked to take the billiard table with him.

During the next year or so, a gradual change took place at school. Mr. Smith, the Latin teacher, was no longer the only male staff member. Teachers who had gone off to war came back to reclaim their jobs. We girls all fell in love with those glamorous returning war heroes. Mr. Henry, the French teacher, had served at Normandy. We pictured him running up the beach, yelling, "*Vous êtes libre! Vous êtes libre!*" We whispered to one another that Mr. Cunningham, who taught English, was an atheist. This was based on the fact that he never led prayers at the morning assembly. It was confirmed when it was his turn to sit at the teachers' table and say grace before we ate our school dinner. We were all electrified when he solemnly intoned:

Oh Lord, we thank you for this food.
Make us, and it, and our digestions good!

Apparently, having a sense of humor was frowned upon by the powers that be. Mr. Cunningham never sat at the teachers' table again. We agreed that this had been a smart move on his part. School dinners were terrible, probably due to shortages of ingredients rather than to the fault of the cook. I can still visualize the bread pudding—lumps of soggy bread with burned raisins sprinkled on top. We called it "Rabbits' Playground."

Although we were now older and more sophisticated, we still organized camping trips to the Chapman farm. The one that stands out in my memory is the year we helped out in a field-burning operation, running along the edge of a field with flaring torches, setting fire to the dry dead grass to encourage new grass to grow. It was wildly exciting, but what made it more memorable was that we were working alongside German soldiers.

Because of the shortage of farm labor, inmates were temporarily released from prisoner-of-war camps to help produce more food for a still-hungry nation. This was probably after the end of the war and the soldiers were waiting for repatriation. When we met them on Betty's father's farm, they didn't seem like the enemy. For one thing, they were young—just boys, a year or two older than we were. Some of them were fifteen or sixteen.

We flirted with them shamelessly. There was, of course, the language barrier. Although they had picked up a few English words, we didn't know any German. It wasn't taught in British schools. But that didn't stop me from asking one of them to teach us to say something in German.

"*Ich liebe dich von ganzem Herzen,*" he said.

I repeated the sentence earnestly. It was much later that I found out I was telling him, "I love you with all my heart!"

Peter, 1948

After the war, when the signs asking if your journey was really necessary had disappeared, we resumed family holidays to the Highlands, but Peter wasn't with us. When he turned 18 in 1946, he was drafted into the army to do his two years of National Service. Mandatory National Service lasted through the 1950s. But even if Peter had been at Mallaig Mhor, we couldn't have captured the magic of those long-ago summers. Ann and I hiked in the hills and swam in the ocean and made collections of wild flowers, but we no longer pretended to be Bonnie Prince Charlie hiding in the heather or staged fights with hermit crabs. We had put away childish things, though I couldn't help feeling that we'd been cheated out of some of our childhood years.

It was harder to deal with the hardships we had to put up with after the war was over than during the war when we were bound together in a common cause. On the other hand, we were so used to dealing with such things as rationing that it had become a way of life. By the time Eleanor and I were sharing a small flat while attending Edinburgh University in the early 1950s, we couldn't remember a time when you didn't need coupons as well as money to buy food.

But those were drab years. When I emigrated to Canada in 1955, ten years after the war ended, it was like suddenly stepping out of a black-and-white world into a technicolor one. I was astonished that cars came in so many different colors.

19

A Place Far Away

The other day I ran into my friend Carolyn and her 4-year-old son. While we were talking, the little boy whispered to his mom, "Is the lady from a place far away?" Despite having lived many more years in Oregon than in Scotland, I still tend to roll my *r's* and people often ask where I'm from. But it wasn't until I began writing these childhood memories that I realized how much my writing career and who I am today are influenced by that "Place Far Away".

    I didn't set out to be a writer. My best subject at school was mathematics. Now when my checkbook doesn't balance, I console myself with the thought that long ago I was the recipient of the John W. Smith Bequest Prize in Mathematics in my final year at Dumfries Academy. Perhaps as a harbinger of what was yet to come, the prize was *A Little Treasury of Modern Poetry.*

    At Edinburgh University I studied botany and genetics. I had a head start in botany from days spent collecting wildflowers in the Boggy Bit and on Highland holidays. Genetics tied in with my liking for numbers. We reared thousands of fruit flies, keeping track of crumpled wings and straight wings, black eyes and red eyes. All this counting prepared me for a job as a statistician at East Malling Research Station in the south of England. This is where I first saw my name in print. I co-authored a scientific paper: *Some Statistical Aspects of a Recent Series of Fruit Tree Red Spider Mite Control Trials*. It makes for really dull reading!

Research at East Malling focused on apple trees. We designed the layout for experimental plots for trees that wouldn't bear results for ten years. I decided I couldn't wait around that long to see if we'd grown a better apple, so I emigrated to Canada in March, 1955.

Perhaps I had inherited the wanderlust gene. My father's brother, Uncle George, spent his adult life in Africa, while my mother's brothers, Uncle Alex and Uncle Lindsey, moved to India and Australia. Peter, after a short stint as a junior journalist at the Edinburgh Evening News—the same newspaper where his grandfather had been the sports editor—headed off to Canada and then moved to the United States. In those days, we traveled by ship. It took me almost a week to cross the Atlantic on the *Empress of France*. Back then places were farther away.

I eventually ended up at a research station in the Okanagan Valley, British Columbia, where I met my future husband, Norm. We spent a few years bouncing around between Oregon, Canada, and England where Norm earned his Ph.D. in entomology and we became the parents of twins, Richard and Judith. We finally put down roots in Corvallis when Norm was offered a position at Oregon State University and I began to write.

Margaret and Norm, September 1956, by Angelyn Voss

Norm's field is aquatic entomology, which turned out to be an ideal occupation for the father of small children. During the sixties, while he was familiarizing himself with the insects of Oregon, we spent our weekends traveling around the state in our blue Volkswagen bus with (by now) four children. We dabbled in ditches and small streams and rivers. Even before Karen started kindergarten she could tell a larval mayfly from a stonefly. We all loved the caddisflies that scuttled about on the streambeds in their little stone houses. In the sixties, we weren't Flower Children; we were Insect Children. And the entire state was my Boggy Bit.

For several years, drawing on my own biology background and Norm's expertise, I wrote articles for children's magazines such as *Ranger Rick* and *Nature and Science*. After consolidating some of these articles into my first book, *Exploring the Insect World*, I turned to writing fiction.

When the children were young I used to tell them stories, just as I had told Ann stories to hurry her along to school. These stories were mostly an attempt to keep them from fighting in the car or careening into the ironing board. Just the sound of me spitting on a hot iron would bring them running from all corners of the house. They'd sit on the floor with upturned faces listening to my "war stories" about creeping into the house next door after the soldiers left and having evacuees live with us—stories that eventually worked their way into *Searching for Shona*. I sometimes claim that the invention of no-iron fabrics finally gave me time to write the stories down.

Writing *Searching for Shona* brought forth many memories, but it turned out that not everything I recalled was accurate. Although I was picturing Lockerbie as the destination for my evacuees, I decided to call the place Canonbie, thinking that was the name of a farm near Lockerbie. It turned out to be the name of another border town. I like to think that it wasn't laziness that led me to using actual names of places. It was more that they added to the authenticity and transported me back to scenes from my childhood. While I was writing *Searching for Shona*, and recalled my childhood fascination with Clairmont House, I never pictured the present owner—or anyone else in Scotland—actually reading my book.

Although most of my early fiction books were set in places I remembered from my childhood, *The Journey of the Shadow Bairns* was based on Norm's family history. On a visit to Canada, my mother-in-law handed me a copy of a letter with the words, "You should write a book about this." The letter had been written by her father, Arthur Black, to his brother back in England after Arthur emigrated to Canada with the Barr colonists in 1903. In it he describes everything from the weather to the price of a horse to the building of his log cabin. My first draft sounded like I was trying to write *Little House in Northern Saskatchewan*, so I started over, sending Elspeth and Robbie off to Canada alone on the ship. This was a journey I could easily imagine. I was suddenly back on the *Empress of France*, pulling out from Liverpool, with the band on the shore playing;

For we're no awa' tae bide awa',
For we're no awa' tae leave ye,

For we're no awa' tae bide awa',
We'll aye come back an' see ye.

As it turned out, although I've been back to Scotland a number of times over the years, I really was awa' tae bide awa'.

On trips back to Scotland, when we visited Smailholm Tower, my father told his grandchildren the same stories he'd told to me as a child. He loved to recall how, in his courting days, he and their grandmother had climbed out onto the tower roof and sat on the ridge watching the sun go down. The children stood wide-eyed as he recited the lines from Sir Walter Scott's *Eve of St. John*:

The sable score of fingers four
Remains on the board impress'd;
And forever more that lady wore
A covering on her wrist.

Then he would tell them the story of Muckle-mooth Meg. Long, long ago, when the laird of Smailholm captured an English raider, he offered to spare the man's life if he would marry the laird's homely daughter, Muckle-mooth Meg. The Englishman took one look at the poor lass and said he'd rather hang. But when he was facing the gallows, he quickly decided he'd be better off married. That particular story stuck in my mind because Peter used to tease me, calling me

Muckle-mooth Meg. When I complained to my parents they just reminded me that sticks and stones will break your bones, but names can never hurt you.

Susan, Judith, Karen, and Richard, Smailholm Tower, 1971

It was one of those picnics at Smailholm Tower that provided me with the opening chapters of *In the Keep of Time*. We had picked up the key at the nearby farmhouse and let ourselves into the tower through the studded oak door. While we stood there in the dim light looking up at the distant roof, a big black bird fluttered down and landed dead at our feet. It had apparently forced its way through a gap in the chicken wire that covered the narrow windows some time earlier and had starved to death. We gave it a decent burial in a rabbit hole. When we returned to Corvallis and I was looking for something to write about, the whole scene came flooding back, along with my father's stories.

To Nowhere and Back began with a question. In the early 1970s, we spent a sabbatical year in Dorset. We rented Random Cottage in the village of Wool, where Susan, our middle daughter, attended the local school, which was celebrating its centennial that year. But why were schools in all the villages around Wool also turning a hundred? The answer lay in the Education Act of 1871, which mandated that all children ages five to thirteen were to attend school. This resulted in a rush to build schools. In my time-slip story, an American girl who is nervous about going to a new school experiences the life of a girl who lived a hundred years earlier—a girl who would be too old to learn to read and write by the time the school was built. While I was writing the book, Old Scrubber Liz of my childhood crept into the story and I found her living in our thatched cottage. When my father read the book, he was surprised to learn that I had encountered Scrubber Liz in our visits to St. Boswells. He had known her as Old Scrubber Liz back when he was a child. I guess "old" is a relative term.

I've been back to Lockerbie several times over the years. The quiet little town has its its own stories, some of them tragic. Lockerbie was suddenly in headlines all over the world in December 1988, when a terrorist bomb brought down Pan Am Flight 103, killing all 259 people on board and 11 people in Lockerbie. I felt the tragedy deeply, personally. I had returned from my mother's funeral the day before on a Pan American flight. I felt as if my past was being ripped to shreds.

Lockerbie has also been on the radar for happier reasons. In the 2014 Winter Olympics in Sochi, Russia, the British men's and women's curling teams both came away with medals. David Murdoch, from Lockerbie, led his team to a silver. Lockerbie natives, Claire Hamilton and Anna Sloan, were on the bronze-winning women's team. Curling is no longer an old man's game—it belongs to the young as well as the old, to girls as well as boys. Children as young as six take curling lessons in the indoor rink across the road from Lockerbie Academy.

Eskrigg Nature Reserve, photo by Lenna Tiryaki

After the ice rink was built in 1966, reed-grass and other vegetation gradually overtook Eskrigg Pond. The pond had been excavated in the mid-nineteenth century to serve as a curling pond and would have disappeared if a pupil at Lockerbie Academy hadn't told his biology teacher, Jim Rae, about this boggy bit on the edge of town. When Jim visited the site he immediately saw its potential, not just for fieldwork with his science classes, but also for the whole community. Three years later, when the reed-grass had been dug out and the sluice gate repaired, the pond came back to life. Today people from all over visit Eskrigg Nature Reserve to enjoy the viewing areas, talks, and woodland paths. They can watch the waterfowl and the happy antics of the numerous red squirrels. And maybe, on a cold winter evening, if they listen hard, they can hear an echo of the hum of those long-ago curling stones.

Smailholm Tower, too, has changed over the years. You no longer pick up a key from Sandyknowe Farm and let yourself in. It is now a 5-star tourist destination. The floors of the upstairs rooms have been rebuilt and glass windows keep out curious birds. One of the rooms houses a lovely exhibit of costumed figures from Sir Walter Scott's ballads. But I'm a little sad that Smailholm is no longer the lonely mysterious tower of my childhood.

Places, like people, each have their own unfolding story. So, I find that while I've been here in Oregon writing this memoir, I've been revisiting a time far away as well as a place far away.

ACKNOWLEDGEMENTS

My heartfelt thanks to my sister, Ann Middleditch, for being such a big part of my story, and to Wendy Madar at Lychgate Press for her ideas and enthusiasm. Thanks to my children and grandchildren for listening to my "war stories" and keeping them alive in my mind. A special thanks to granddaughters Gillian and Jena for their ideas for the cover and to Fiona for finding the missing file. Also thanks to Karen Stephenson and Frances Chapple for their copy-editing skills, and to Norm for being a patient listener and careful critic.

At first, I didn't know I was working on a book. It started out as episodes I read to the Thursday Writing Group. Their response to my childhood adventures kept me going. I am grateful to young Henry West Holthoff for providing me with the title without even reading the book. And a special thanks to Nancy Matsumoto for all the rides she has given me on dark Thursday nights.

Margaret Anderson was born and educated in Scotland, and graduated from Edinburgh University. Before she took up writing for children she worked as a biologist and statistician. She is the author of 25 books ranging from nature activity and biographies of famous scientists to historical fiction and time-travel adventures. Anderson lives in Corvallis, Oregon, with her husband, an entomologist. Insects are featured in several of her books.

Made in the USA
San Bernardino, CA
22 November 2017